THE SATURDAYS
OUR STORY

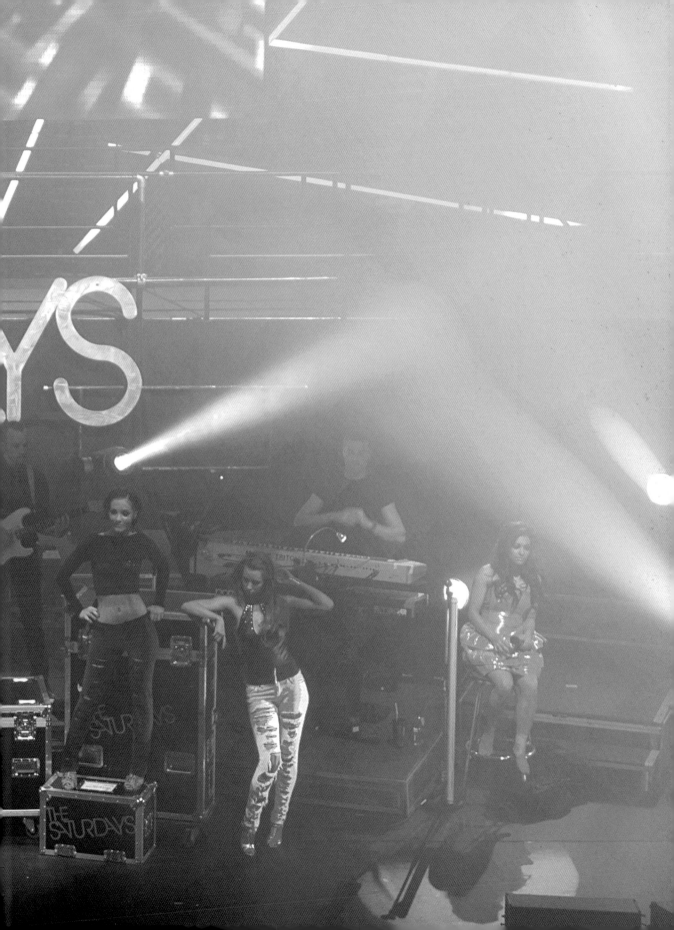

OUR STORY

We can't believe that it's been more than three
years since we became a band – The Saturdays!
It seems even more incredible to think that at the time of
writing we've notched up two top-ten albums, six top-ten
singles and our own sell-out nationwide tour. We never
dreamed life could be this good!

This is the story of our amazing journey so far; how
we grew up and worked hard to achieve our goals;
the highs and lows along the way; the lessons we've
learned; how we got together and became the best of
friends; how *fantastic* it is to perform live on tour; how we
developed the sound of The Saturdays; how to work the
red carpet (well, we try); the boys we've loved (and still
love!); and much, much more! It's not been easy to get
to where we are today, but it's been worth it, every step
of the way.

We hope that this book inspires you to believe in yourself
and make your dreams come true. We'd like to dedicate
it to everyone who believed in and supported us.

Lots of love

First published in Great Britain in 2010 by Hodder & Stoughton
An Hachette UK company

1

Copyright © The Saturdays 2010

A CIP catalogue record for this title is available from
the British Library.

ISBN 978 1 444 70554 6

Typeset in SWISS by Max Miedinger

Printed and bound by in Italy by Graphicom Srl

Text design by Zip Design

Hodder & Stoughton policy is to use papers that are natural,
renewable and recyclable products and made from wood grown
in sustainable forests. The logging and manufacturing processes are
expected to conform to the environmental regulations of
the country of origin.

Hodder & Stoughton Ltd
338 Euston Road
London NW1 3BH
www.hodder.co.uk

THE SATURDAYS STARTING OUT

WHERE DO POP STARS COME FROM? ARE THEY BORN THAT WAY, OR ARE THEY MADE? WE CAME FROM DIFFERENT PLACES AND BACKGROUNDS, BUT IS THERE SOMETHING WE ALL HAVE IN COMMON? AND DOES DESTINY PLAY A PART?

Frankie — As a kid, I hated Sunday. It was the most boring day of the week – even thinking about it now makes me want to fall asleep! My mum and dad are really into sport and they used to spend Sundays watching car racing – zzzzzzz . . . ! So I was thrilled when they let me audition for a local stage school, where I could spend the whole of Sunday dancing, singing and acting. I was nine years old. I'd been having dance lessons at our nearby community centre for six years, ever since I was three.

At the school open day, I looked around me in amazement; a whole new world of possibility opened up to me. On the stage in the main hall, some girls were singing and dancing. One of them really stood out: she was very pretty and a great dancer. She's brilliant, I thought. I want to be up there doing that too!

I couldn't wait for my audition. I was desperate to start attending the school, but it was my first ever audition and I was scared. Trembling, I sang a song from *Joseph and the Amazing Technicolor Dreamcoat*, which I'd learned with the school choir.

Soon afterwards, without knowing if I'd got in or not, I went on holiday. It was a really big deal when I returned and found out that I'd been accepted. I was over the moon!

On my first Sunday at the school, I spotted the girl I'd seen up on stage at the open day. A little later on, she introduced herself as Rochelle. I had no idea that our lives and futures would be so connected, but from that day on she and I have been really good friends.

Rochelle — I was constantly singing and dancing when I was young. I started at four years old and I've never stopped. After school, I would rush home and go off to dance, and I danced all weekend.

I attended Collins Performing Arts (CPA), which is local to me in Essex. When my mum couldn't afford for me to attend, she worked there in order to pay the fees. Sometimes I taught the little kids basic ballet: 'Good toes; naughty toes.' Together, me and my mum would earn enough to pay for me to go to classes on Sunday. It meant so much to me, I would have done anything.

I WANTED TO BE A POP STAR FROM THE AGE OF SIX.
I DON'T KNOW WHO OR WHAT INSPIRED IT.

MOLLIE

Una — I was a small, really skinny child, a very bad eater, and my hair was dull and thin. I can still remember my mother trying to feed me by pretending the fork was an aeroplane. It wasn't very successful . . . 'I want sweets! I want sweets,' I'd cry. My poor grandfather, Dan-Joe, who'd had two hip replacements, had to walk down the road to buy me sweets because I was craving them all the time. I also used to go around the house complaining, 'Mammy, I'm bored! I'm bored!'

Then, when I was six, my mum saw an advertisement in the local paper for a swimming club and immediately thought it could be the answer. I don't know why, because my most memorable experience of the water had not been very pleasant, to say the least. It dated back to when I was four and my mum and I were in the showers at the swimming pool.
— 'Where is your sister?' my mum asked.
— 'She's still in the swimming pool,' I said. 'I'll go and get her.' The next minute, I jumped in the pool without my armbands and started to drown. I still remember it so well. Panicking, I kept coming up for big gulps of air and then sinking again, until the lifeguard eventually pulled me out. I didn't want to go near the water after that.

But I got over my fear two years later when my mum sent me for swimming lessons. I went on to be the fastest nine-year-old swimmer in Ireland! I swam for my school, Presentation Convent, Thurles, and won the All-Ireland Gold Championship when I was nine. I swam fifty metres in thirty-seven seconds – I still feel very proud of that!

Swimming makes you extremely hungry, so I started eating loads. My hair improved and I began to grow. I was never bored again, because I went swimming every day after school. If I hadn't done it, I reckon I'd still be really small and scrawny, so thank goodness my mum saw that ad!

> ## I WAS A SMALL, REALLY SKINNY CHILD, A VERY BAD EATER, AND MY HAIR WAS DULL AND THIN. I CAN STILL REMEMBER MY MOTHER TRYING TO FEED ME BY PRETENDING THE FORK WAS AN AEROPLANE.
> UNA

Mollie — I wanted to be a pop singer for as long as I can remember! No one in my family shared my passion for singing and dancing. It came completely out of the blue! One of my sisters is a lawyer; the other is a banker. My dad is an accountant, and my mum was a photographer, so when I began saying I wanted to be a pop singer, no one took me seriously; they all thought I would grow out of it!

My earliest memories are of Kylie – I never knew any nursery rhymes, but I knew all the words to Kylie's album aged three! 'I Should Be So Lucky' was always rockin' in the car!

Take That were my next favourite; man those boys could dance! I remember watching their 'Never Forget' video, which is a montage of the band over the years, playing arenas, meeting fans and travelling on the tour bus – I thought their lives looked absolutely amazing and I couldn't get it out of my

head! For someone who spent every spare minute singing and dancing around the house, this was the ultimate goal! I would spend hours and hours singing with my hairbrush and practising in the mirror! Cringe I know, but I'm afraid it's true!

> ## THE MOMENT I SAW BRITNEY, I SAID, 'THIS IS WHAT I HAVE TO DO.'
> MOLLIE

I didn't get really serious, though, until Britney appeared, when I was eleven years old. The moment I saw Britney, I said, 'This is what I have to do.' I absolutely loved her and everything about her. I wanted to be her. I had pictures of her all over my bedroom walls, I knew her lyrics, and I continually studied her music videos. I was a massive, massive fan.

I also felt that our personalities were quite similar. Back then, she was a good girl, and I was a good girl. Her mum was her best friend. 'Oh my goodness', I thought, '*my* mum is *my* best friend!' Britney talked to her mum about everything, and I talked to my mum about everything. She was hard-working and so was I. 'If she can do it, I can do it,' I thought. And that was it!

> ## I ABSOLUTELY LOVED HER AND EVERYTHING ABOUT HER. I WANTED TO BE HER.
> MOLLIE

Vanessa — I've loved singing all my life. I wouldn't shut up, even when I was five years old. We lived in Somerset at the time and my mum and dad would drive me and my sister to singing lessons at the Sylvia Young Theatre School in London on a Saturday. We used to set off at six in the morning!

We did that for a year and then my mum persuaded my dad to move to East London, so that it would be easier for me to go to the Saturday classes. I didn't appreciate their sacrifice at the time. It was just a case of 'Cool, we are moving. Great!' Now I realise that they did it for me and I have to thank them for that.

I think they agreed to do it because I would never stop singing. By the age of seven, I was belting out Céline Dion songs. Crazy now to think of this little girl singing about big romances, but I loved it.

> ## BY THE AGE OF SEVEN, I WAS BELTING OUT CÉLINE DION SONGS
> VANESSA

Frankie — Until I went to Sunday stage school, dancing had just been a bit of fun for me, but now I began to take my lessons much more seriously. I did acting, singing and lots of different kinds of dancing classes, not just jazz, ballet and tap. I loved every minute. As time went on, I started going up for parts in shows and adverts. I usually did well and often made it to the final audition, but I never actually got the part. It was so frustrating!

I became convinced that I wasn't good enough and needed more acting lessons. 'You don't need extra lessons,' my drama teacher assured me, but I was determined. I begged my mum to let me have two private acting classes a week and eventually she gave in.

The stage school held a summer camp in the holidays, which you could attend for a full week. One year, I won a contest for my performance of Macavity from *Cats*. My mum taught me the song, choreographed it and made me an all-in-one furry suit, which I can't imagine her doing now, funnily enough! I'm not sure I can imagine wearing an all-in-one furry suit, either!

AS TIME WENT ON, I STARTED GOING UP FOR PARTS IN SHOWS AND ADVERTS. I USUALLY DID WELL AND OFTEN MADE IT TO THE FINAL AUDITION, BUT I NEVER ACTUALLY GOT THE PART. IT WAS SO FRUSTRATING!

FRANKIE

Winning the competition was a really big deal, but I still wasn't getting any parts in the shows I auditioned for. I got down to the last three for the main child part in a musical called *Whistle Down The Wind* , but missed out; then in the summer holidays before I went to secondary school, when I was twelve, I went for the main part in *Annie* and made it to the final audition.

After trying and trying and being called back again and again, I didn't get it. I was devastated. I had been so close to landing the best part of all time! I was gutted at the time, but looking back, I realise that it was probably a lucky escape, because I would have had to start my new school with a ginger bob that really didn't suit me!

Vanessa — It's funny that one of Frankie's first big performances was from the musical *Cats*, because, when I was nine, I was given a singing part in a Sylvia Young Summer School production of the musical. Mine wasn't a big success, though – I had a bit of a solo and then forgot my words!

My mum still has the video at home. It is really embarrassing and I just feel so sorry for myself when I watch it. I'm standing there and singing and all of a sudden my mind goes blank. I look absolutely petrified. It's awful!

Still, I loved being on stage; I always felt at home there. Around that time, I was given a Walkman cassette player and I used to go to sleep listening to Michael Jackson's *Thriller* every night. I loved learning his songs and I was mad about Céline Dion. I'm not as crazy about her as I once was, but I still always think, 'You know what? You are amazing!' She is one of the people who made me want to do this and I'll always love her. I love Mariah Carey and Whitney Houston too – all the big stars.

When I was ten, I was one of the original cast of the revival of the musical *The King and I*. It wasn't a big part, but it gave me a lot of confidence and probably helped me get the part of the young Nala in *The Lion King* the following year. I had the best time ever playing Nala. I met some great people and many are still my good friends now.

We were very well looked after. Our dressing room was just for kids and they wanted to make it fun. It was done up like a jungle, and it was full of framed consoles on the walls and there were loads of games to play on them. We spent a lot of our time in there drawing and colouring and doing other cool stuff. I really got on with a boy called Michael, who was playing Simba, and I've kind of grown up with him since then. We always used to mess about together and now we've become really good friends.

> I USED TO GO TO SLEEP LISTENING TO MICHAEL JACKSON'S *THRILLER* EVERY NIGHT. I LOVED LEARNING HIS SONGS . . .
> VANESSA

The head teacher of my primary school was very supportive and allowed me to go home from school early on the days I had a matinée, once or twice a week. If I was only doing the evening show, I didn't have to leave early, because the show started at 7 p.m.

Whenever one of the cast or crew was leaving one of the shows, everyone would gather at a nearby jazz bar and sing songs. All of the young ones would get together and practise for ages before a night like that. It was amazing, definitely one of the best times of my life. It was a six-month contract, but they liked me and my friend Michael so much that they asked us to stay on. I was thrilled because I didn't want to leave. I was there for a year in all. They had to boot me out in the end!

Frankie — Soon after I was turned down for *Annie*, there was a whole load of stuff on TV about an open audition for young performers. It was something to do with S Club 7, a pop group I loved at the time. Because it was an open audition, though, I knew anybody could go along.

> STILL, I LOVED BEING ON STAGE; I ALWAYS FELT AT HOME THERE.
> VANESSA

— 'I'm not going,' I told my best friend, Matt. 'There will be thousands of people there. It'll be chaos.'
— 'Go on, give it a try anyway,' Matt said. 'It sounds like a really good opportunity.'
— 'Well, maybe . . .' I replied. That evening at my house, I discussed it with Rochelle. We ummed and aahed for a while. 'Shall we just do it?' I said suddenly. 'Shall we just go?'
— 'All right!' she replied, giggling. 'We'd better learn some S Club 7 songs right now!'

The next morning, we got up very early and our mums drove us to the audition in Wembley. When we arrived, there were kids everywhere, looking really done up, practising their dance routines in the queue. We gave each other worried looks. Oh dear! We felt very underdressed in our jeans and vest tops. Plus, we didn't have a dance routine and didn't really know the songs.
— 'What's this audition actually for, anyway?' Rochelle asked.
— 'I'm not really sure!' I said, laughing.

THE ONLY THING WE KNEW WAS THAT, IF WE GOT THROUGH, WE WOULD SPEND A NIGHT ON STAGE AT WEMBLEY SUPPORTING S CLUB 7 ON THE CARNIVAL TOUR.

FRANKIE

After driving all that way, there was no point going home, so we went through the auditions and made it to the end of the day. What was it all about? The only thing we knew was that, if we got through, we would spend a night on stage at Wembley supporting S Club 7 on the Carnival Tour.

Two weeks later, we were called back. After more auditions, they called out the names of the people who had been selected. Rochelle's name was called first. It was being filmed for a CBBC documentary and you can tell when you watch it back that she was trying not to look too pleased in case I didn't get called. Then they called out my name and she started jumping up and down. You can see our mums jumping around madly in the background too!

We were very excited about performing at Wembley with S Club 7. Then it turned out that S Club's manager, Simon Fuller, had decided that he wanted to form us into a young, new pop group. I guess that was the idea all along, but he had been waiting to see how the auditions went and who emerged from them before making his final decision. When he saw us, he said,

— 'OK, let's do it.'

It was weird. Suddenly, we were in a pop group.

— 'OK, then, thanks!' we said. We stopped off at McDonald's on the way home to celebrate.

Rochelle — It was so random how we got into S Club Juniors. I was watching CBBC and saw something about a competition to support S Club 7 and sing at Wembley Arena for one night.

— 'Mum, this looks so much fun! Please take me,' I said. Frankie came too, at the last minute. We didn't know about the band until the final week, when Simon Fuller came down and said,

— 'I've found a band that I want to put together here.'

— 'Please let me be a part of it, Mum!' I pleaded.

— 'If you don't let me, I won't like you, for ever and ever!'

She was quite sceptical at first. I had just turned twelve and to send me out to work, so to speak, was a bit daunting.

I was quite an old twelve-year-old and I've always been mature, but she was still frightened. Thankfully, she felt reassured when she checked it all out, so she gave in, even though it felt like letting her baby go.

I'm very close to my mum. We are so tight. I tell her everything, literally. People say, 'Would you really tell your mum that?' Yes, I would! She is a young mum

IF YOU BELIEVE
IN YOURSELF,
THEN YOU FEEL
CONFIDENT AND
COME ACROSS
AS CONFIDENT.
IF YOU FEEL
GOOD YOU'RE
AUTOMATICALLY
MORE CONFIDENT
SO IT'S WORTH
MAKING
AN EFFORT.
VANESSA

THE SATURDAYS "ISSUES"

HRS		MIN		SEC		FRS	

DF

DIR: PETRO

37.5 FPS

SCENE		TAKE			ROLL	

CAM: DENIS CROSSAN

DIRECTOR		CAMERA			DATE
DCODE	TS-1	D...CKE INC.			13-11-08

and we do a lot together. I'm very lucky with my mum. I don't remember my dad being around much; I didn't really know what it was like to have a regular dad at home. When I was younger, it used to upset me, but I don't know any different now. I'm sure it would have been nice sometimes but it doesn't bother me, especially since I've moved out, bought my own house and own a dog. That's enough for me. I know my dad, but I choose not to spend time with him.

He and mum split up when I was very young. My mum never said anything bad about him in front of me. She wanted to let me form my own opinions. I started seeing him every weekend when I was about five. Then he met someone else and started a new family and I felt I wasn't wanted.

My mum met someone else and had my sister, Emily, when I was five. Emily and I used to fight like cat and dog when we were younger, but we get on really well now. She often comes to stay over at my house, whereas before I didn't even want her in my bedroom. It's so nice how our relationship has developed.

> ALTHOUGH WE WORKED IN LONDON, I WAS OFTEN ABLE TO POP HOME TO ENJOY MUM'S COOKING OR TO STAY.
> ROCHELLE

Frankie — S Club Juniors were together for four years, from 2001 to 2005, by which time the name had changed to S Club 8. It was an amazing time for me. People didn't expect the group to catch on, but we did really well. We went on two tours, the first time supporting S Club 7 and the second time on a joint tour called S Club United. By the second tour, we had released two albums and eight singles. We were the first British pop group to get four number twos in a row, I think! We also did a TV drama called *I Dream*, which was filmed in Barcelona over three months.

I only remember the good stuff, because there wasn't much that was bad. We were well looked after and had chaperones with us all the time.

> I GREW USED TO BEING AWAY FROM HOME AND BEING LOOKED AFTER BY OTHER PEOPLE.
> FRANKIE

The rules were very strict: we had to do fifteen hours of schoolwork a week, so we had tutors to teach us. Sometimes we'd be up at 4 or 5 a.m. to perform on *SMTV Live* or *CD:UK* and then we'd go back and do schoolwork afterwards, which was the boring bit!

I grew used to being away from home and being looked after by other people. After a while, it seemed normal. The band and the people we worked with were like a big family.

I'm still in touch with all of them. (Actually, I count myself lucky that I did stay in contact, because being in S Club Juniors ultimately led to being in the Saturdays, who are part of the same record label, Polydor.)

Four of us were from Essex, near enough to London to be able to go home a lot.

The other four weren't so lucky: they were from further away and had to live in a house in London, so they were always apart from their parents. Of course, when we were on tour or filming abroad, none of us managed to get home. Sometimes you could be away for as long as a month.

Our parents couldn't travel with us, partly because they had jobs to do and partly because there were so many of them that I think it was easier to keep them at a distance! It was quite hard for them, perhaps harder for them than it was for us. Obviously, there were times when we felt tired or ill and then we'd miss home, but I found it much easier to be away from home when I was younger than I do now! I was a bit more oblivious back then. I was also a lot more disciplined.

Rochelle — Although we worked in London, I was often able to pop home to enjoy my mum's cooking or to stay. Whenever I talk to Mum about those days, she says that accepting that your twelve-year-old daughter is going to work is just the weirdest thing. Thank God she let me do it, because I wouldn't be in the Saturdays if I hadn't been in S Club Juniors. She did the right thing, bless her. She trusted me and she trusted the people around me.

Everything was catered for and cautiously monitored. Our management company was careful to please our parents and make sure we were happy. We had chaperones and we had the same driver every day, because putting your child in a cab on their own is a big deal for some parents. The driver I had is now a family friend.

We could only work a certain number of hours a day. As soon as it was approaching the last half an hour, our chaperones would say, 'Right, that's it. They are done for today.' We would leave immediately afterwards.

I thought that life would be just as easy when I first joined the Saturdays. I couldn't wait to get back into it. It didn't take long to realise that, because I was a child, I had experienced the glorified version of life as a pop star. It's not the same now. We work our butts off!

Una — I come from a small town called Thurles in Co Tipperary and I didn't have the opportunities available to girls who live in or near a big city. There weren't any stage schools nearby. I did everything going, though. I went to a local ballet class, run by a lady called Pauline Dwan, every Saturday; I also tried Irish dancing, but was really bad at it!

I GREW USED
TO BEING AWAY
FROM HOME AND
BEING LOOKED
AFTER BY OTHER
PEOPLE. AFTER
A WHILE, IT
SEEMED NORMAL.
THE BAND AND
THE PEOPLE WE
WORKED WITH
WERE LIKE A
BIG FAMILY.
FRANKIE

I grew up in a very musical family and I always loved music. My uncle, Declan Nerney, is a really famous Irish country singer and I often went to see him perform.

My mother was also a singer. She used to be semi-professional back when she was a student nurse. She played guitar in a band and she taught me guitar. She listened to country music constantly when I was little, so my roots are in country music, really.

We didn't have MTV when I was little, so I used to listen to pop music on the radio, in particular *Ireland's Top 30* hosted by Larry Gogan on 2FM. I would sit by the radio with a blank tape waiting for my favourite songs to come on, so I could record them. Then I could listen back to them whenever I wanted to.

The first two records I ever bought were Madonna's *True Blue* and Michael Jackson's *Bad*, both on cassette. They cost me about £6, which was money well spent as I played them all the time. Before long I was singing and dancing along to every word of every song on those two albums.

> # I THOUGHT THAT LIFE WOULD BE JUST AS EASY WHEN I FIRST JOINED THE SATURDAYS. I COULDN'T WAIT TO GET BACK INTO IT.
> ROCHELLE

I gave up swimming when I was thirteen because I had no swimming club to train with any more. Around this time, I fell in love with playing the guitar. One of the first tunes I played was a song I wrote after my grandfather died; it was called 'I Miss You'. I knew three chords – D, G and C – and you can write any song with those chords. In fact, some of the most beautiful songs have been composed using just three chords.

As a teenager, I wrote songs and poetry to express my feelings. Emotions are huge at that age, probably because you're experiencing everything for the first time. Love, longing, hurt and heartbreak are incredibly strong feelings at any age, but when you're a teenager, you think the world is going to end when someone breaks up with you; it's a much bigger deal. I found it helped to get it out in poetry and songs. I still find now that writing things down is a brilliant way to get them off my chest; it's very therapeutic.

> # AS A TEENAGER, I WROTE SONGS AND POETRY TO EXPRESS MY FEELINGS.
> UNA

Mollie — When I was six we went on a family skiing holiday and, so that we didn't spend the first few days standing around freezing, my sisters and I had some lessons at our local dry ski slope before we went. I *loved* it! I was going through a phase where I was a real tomboy – I dressed in tracksuits and T-shirts all the time, and wore a cap and was very brave, so the speed and scariness of the sport was so exciting; I was soon in their race team.

At seven I was the youngest but the fastest girl in the area and by age eleven I was in the British Children's Ski Team. It wasn't always as glamorous as it sounds! There was little time spent on actual snow – most of it was on artificial slopes in England in the pouring rain but then I won a scholarship to the British Ski Academy and went off to live in France for a while which was fun.

It was hard work, though: up at 6 a.m. every morning because I had to be on the top of the mountain by 7 a.m. Then I would do race practice all morning, school all afternoon and then homework. But my mum always let me watch a Britney video before bedtime and then I could go to bed dreaming of how my own video would be when I grew up!

Sometimes I would jump into bed with my mum and tell her my plans – how on tour I would enter from under the stage – when that actually happened at Wembley last year I nearly cried remembering how I used to dream about it!

I was lucky enough to be part of the England Ski Team and race in Europe and America for my country but I knew it wasn't where my dreams were – my coach used to say,
— 'Mollie – if you really want to be the best, you need to concentrate!' and I used to think,
— 'I don't really – I just want to be a singer and dancer and perform on the biggest stage in the world!'
He knew really – he's still my friend and is thrilled for me that my dream has come true!

Vanessa — Sylvia Young was the school I wanted to go to after my primary school. In my head, I wasn't going to another school. Even though I hated it at times, I was aware that I was lucky to be there.

It was the kind of school where kids sang and danced in the corridors. I also sang in the corridors, but I wasn't a stage-school brat like some of the others. I was quite naughty at school, though. I was always being told off for talking and gossiping in the corner. If it was a singing lesson, then I'd be fine, but often I didn't concentrate in the other lessons. I wasn't interested in anything other than singing.

Every time I went to a music lesson, I was in heaven. I didn't enjoy music studies, though – the theory side of music, which we did for GCSE. I was OK at reading music – it took me a while, but I got into it. Then all of a sudden we had to compose our own piece of music. I ended up composing a stream of random sounds and

I DIDN'T WANT TO BE A DANCER; THERE WAS ONLY ONE PLACE I WANTED TO GO TO AND THAT WAS THE BRIT SCHOOL, A LEADING PERFORMING-ARTS COLLEGE. I WAS GUTTED WHEN I DIDN'T GET IN. IT SHATTERED MY CONFIDENCE.

VANESSA

somehow I got away with it! I had no idea what I was doing; my style was experimental.

The school was in Marylebone, Central London, and I lived in Stratford, in the East End. I had a lot of friends who lived in Essex, and some of my friends were from Leyton, so we would meet up every morning and get the Central Line on the Underground together. We were the Central Line Club. I remember getting told off in a school assembly after someone complained about our behaviour on the train. There were ten or twelve of us from stage school singing really loudly all the way to Marylebone. We got into so much trouble the next day!

> I WAS QUITE NAUGHTY
> AT SCHOOL, THOUGH.
> I WAS ALWAYS BEING TOLD
> OFF FOR TALKING AND
> GOSSIPING IN THE CORNER.
> VANESSA

I was on a half-scholarship and there were a few times when the school threatened to take it away from me. I was bad but not too extreme. A few of my friends were expelled, but I managed to avoid it.

When it was time to leave, everybody else seemed to be going to dance college, but I didn't want to be a dancer; there was only one place I wanted to go to and that was the BRIT School, a leading performing-arts college. I was gutted when I didn't get in. It shattered my confidence.

Looking back, I probably wasn't called for an audition at the college because my application was so bad. I thought I'd given it my all, but obviously not. 'OK,' I decided, 'I'm just going to do loads of auditions and get somewhere that way.'

Una — My father is a GP and my mother is a practice nurse, so they put a lot of emphasis on education. They were the proudest and most encouraging parents in the world, but they wanted me to have something to fall back on if my music didn't work out. My uncle always encouraged my songwriting, but he suggested exploring other careers as well. — 'Listen, music is a tough road,' he warned.

When I was sixteen, I played the part of 'the Duchess' in the school's production of the musical *Me and My Girl*. My music teacher, Mrs Doyle encouraged my songwriting and guitar playing and I performed my own songs for my leaving certificate music exam, achieving a higher level grade A.

Overall I got really good exam results and honours in my Leaving Certificate, which you take at the end of secondary school in Ireland, so I had the option of doing anything I wanted. I didn't know what I wanted to do, though – apart from singing, of course. I was attracted to nursing, partly because of my family's medical background and also because my mother had told me so many stories about having fun as a young nurse. So I applied to train as a nurse.

As I left the house for my nursing interview, my mother took one look at me and said,

MY UNCLE ALWAYS ENCOURAGED MY SONGWRITING, BUT HE SUGGESTED EXPLORING OTHER CAREERS AS WELL. 'LISTEN, MUSIC IS A TOUGH ROAD,' HE WARNED

UNA

— 'You look more like an fashion buyer than a nurse.' I had slapped on loads of make-up and tied my hair up in a little bun. 'They probably won't take you seriously,' she added.

She was right. I failed the interview, which should have been enough to put me off, but I was devastated!

— 'I'd be such a good nurse,' I kept saying.

I took a year out and did a secretarial course. I'm really good at organisation; I reckon I'd be a great PA. I worked as a medical secretary for a while after that. I liked the medical aspect of the job because I had all the knowledge and knew the lingo through my parents. Next I tried primary-school teaching and then I applied to be a nurse again. I did nursing for a year and a half and just hated it. Eventually, I hurt my back and used it as an excuse to get out. 'I can't lift patients when I've got this back pain,' I protested. I was diagnosed with sciatica and given anti-inflammatory medicine, but I didn't get better because my mind didn't want my back to recover and go back to nursing. My back's fine now!

I got out of nursing when I was twenty-one and decided to go for it with music. I was determined to make it work.

— 'All right,' my Mam said. 'Give it five years and see how you get on.'

VANESSA

VANESSA WHITE

TRY AND BELIEVE IN YOURSELF A LITTLE BIT MORE. IF YOU BELIEVE IN YOURSELF, THEN YOU FEEL CONFIDENT AND YOU COME ACROSS AS CONFIDENT. SOMETIMES I HAVE NO IDEA WHERE I FIND MY CONFIDENCE! IF YOU FEEL GOOD, YOU'RE AUTOMATICALLY MORE CONFIDENT, SO IT'S WORTH MAKING AN EFFORT.

AGE — 22
BIRTH — 30 OCTOBER 1989
SIGN — SCORPIO
FROM — SOMERSET

How do you boost your confidence when you're feeling low? — Try and believe in yourself a little bit more. If you believe in yourself, then you feel confident and you come across as confident. Sometimes I have no idea where I find my confidence! If you feel good, you're automatically more confident, so it's worth making an effort. When I'm dressed up to go on stage and I think I look good, I feel confident. I've always loved dressing up. Some days I like to be hippy and that's when I wear my leather hairbands and floral outfits. Other days I wear a little dress with tights and chuck on a pair of boots. At the moment, I am wearing whatever I can find on my floor. I put on anything I can find and hope it works.

Most embarrassing moment — Running down the escalator to catch my train and falling on my face . . . It was peak time as well!

Interesting fact — My uncle used to own a Filipino airline, and, when I was little, I joined a song-and-dance group that appeared at his airline promotions. We would dress in traditional dress and do traditional dances and I remember singing songs in Filipino. We went to Switzerland, Paris, all over the place! It sounds crazy now, and I was the youngest member! Funnily enough, Mutya Buena was in the group at the same time, before she joined the Sugababes.

Would you kiss on a first date? — Hmm, I don't know. I liked to keep them guessing for a few days, maybe even a couple of weeks. In the past I've been known to not even answer the phone! Oh, yes, I did all of that. We all did it once, when we were on tour. We didn't answer the phone to our boyfriends the whole night. Then we went to bed, set an alarm, woke up in the middle of the night and called them, saying, 'Hi. Sorry, we went out. We've only just got in now.' The girls are going to kill me for admitting that! Sussed!

I AM THE . . .
SLOW . . .
MEMBER OF
THE BAND!
I NEVER SEEM
TO KNOW
WHAT'S
GOING ON;
SOMEONE HAS
TO SAY IT, LIKE,
FIFTY TIMES TO
DRUM IT IN!

WHEN I'M DRESSED UP TO GO ON STAGE AND I THINK
I LOOK GOOD, I FEEL CONFIDENT. I'VE ALWAYS LOVED
DRESSING UP. SOME DAYS I LIKE TO BE A HIPPY AND
THAT'S WHEN I WEAR MY LEATHER HAIRBANDS AND
FLORAL OUTFITS.

What would you wear on a first date? — I met
Adam, my last boyfriend, in the summer. I felt gross
because I'd just come from a dance rehearsal with
the girls. I was wearing a vest top, a little flowery
skirt and a pair of flip-flops. 'Whatever,' I thought. 'If
you like me, you like me. If you don't, just forget it!'
I wouldn't have wanted him to think that I had made
an effort, either!

Have you ever had your heart broken? —
Growing up, there were times when I felt rejected,
but I don't think I ever had my heart broken. I'm quite
good at getting over that kind of thing, as long as it's
nothing too important. I'm lucky in that way, I guess,
I can bounce back and turn things round. The one
time I really remember feeling upset over a guy,
I managed to turn the tables, somehow or other.
Then he was the heartbroken one. Yes!

Are you a good shopper? — I'm the worst
shopper ever, although I love shopping. I don't try
things on because I know what I like, I know what
size I am, and I know how I want something to fit.
I hate changing rooms. I only go into a changing
room if I absolutely have to, because I get really hot
and bothered in there. Usually, I just see something
I like, pick it up, buy it, realise what I've done and
then beat myself up about how much I've spent!
I'm just lucky that it often turns out to be something
I really love. Occasionally something doesn't look
as nice as I think it should, but then I end up doing
something to it and wearing it anyway.

I HATE CHANGING
ROOMS. I ONLY GO INTO
A CHANGING ROOM IF
I ABSOLUTELY HAVE TO,
BECAUSE I GET REALLY
HOT AND BOTHERED
IN THERE.

Are you a party animal? — I'm not sure. I go
through different phases. One week I'll feel like
going out every night. I definitely have that side
to me. But there's another side that just prefers
to sit at home and be on my own.

Red-carpet tips? — I'm awful on the red carpet
and I'm awful with paps! I can't stand there and
pose and smile. I just can't do it! I cringe and feel
very shy. I make myself do it when I'm with the
girls but, if I'm pictured on my own, I always look
miserable because I'm so embarrassed or I'm
trying to avoid the camera. If I've had a few drinks,
I know I'll be pulling a funny face, so I try and look
the other way. Una is amazing; she has perfected
the pout. I just can't do it. I don't know why. I need
to learn from Una!

'I'm awful on the red carpet and I'm awful with paps!'

Favourite items in my wardrobe:
—
Lol! I don't have any... I get bored sooo easily.

Relationship advice
—
I don't think I ever had my heart broken. I'm quite good at getting over that kind of thing, as long as it's nothing too important.

Favourite Saturdays single?
—
I love them all, but 'Forever Is Over' is definitely one of my favourites. We all loved it when we first heard it. We couldn't wait to record it.

Worst fashion disaster
—

The worst time was when we went to the High School Musical première wearing different-coloured dresses. They were shiny like PVC — basically bin bags in different colours! Oh God, it was so embarrassing! Actually, I remember that I wasn't bothered at the time. It was Frankie who said they were awful. But now, when I look back, I'm appalled!

Fashion advice
—

I wouldn't say I had a particular style or anything. I just pick up what I like and hope that it works!

Five words that best describe me:
—
Stubborn
Fun
Crazy
Friendly
Slow

ONE WEEK
I'LL FEEL LIKE
GOING OUT
EVERY NIGHT.
I DEFINITELY
HAVE THAT
SIDE TO ME.
BUT THERE'S
ANOTHER SIDE
THAT JUST
PREFERS TO SIT
AT HOME AND
BE ON MY OWN.

I'M THE WORST SHOPPER EVER, ALTHOUGH I LOVE SHOPPING. I DON'T TRY THINGS ON BECAUSE I KNOW WHAT I LIKE, I KNOW WHAT SIZE I AM, AND I KNOW HOW I WANT SOMETHING TO FIT.

On my iPod — I have one, but I don't really have any songs on it because I can't be bothered to sit at home and put them all on. Maybe I should just give my ipod to my brother, as it's just sitting there! Mostly I love my old-school R&B.

- Stevie Wonder
- Whitney Houston
- Céline Dion
- Beyoncé
- Alicia Keys
- Chaka Khan
- Jill Scott
- Christina Aguilera

Favourite Saturdays video? — It was fun making the 'Forever Is Over' video. We shot it in a warehouse and it involved quite a bit of acting.

Favourite Saturdays single? — I love them all, but 'Forever Is Over' is definitely one of my favourites. We all loved it when we first heard it. We couldn't wait to record it.

Wardrobe malfunction? — At the 2010 Brit Awards, I wore a partially see-through black dress. At first, my boobs were hidden by the bit of the dress that wasn't see-through. Unfortunately, after a few drinks, they had moved, but I hadn't realised! I confidently walked out of the building thinking everything was great, only for everyone to see my boobs. It was all over the papers the next day. I was so embarrassed that I didn't leave the house! My phone was ringing all day, but I didn't want to talk to anyone. It was awful and I was depressed about it for a while, but I'm over it now.

IT WAS FUN MAKING THE 'FOREVER IS OVER' VIDEO. WE SHOT IT IN A WAREHOUSE AND IT INVOLVED QUITE A BIT OF ACTING

THE SATURDAYS
CHASING DREAMS

GETTING OUT THERE AND TRYING TO GET NOTICED IS A REAL CHALLENGE. YOU CAN'T AVOID THE REJECTIONS AND KNOCKBACKS. YOU KNOW YOU SHOULD TAKE EACH DISAPPOINTMENT WITH A PINCH OF SALT, BUT THAT CAN BE HARDER THAN IT SOUNDS. WE'VE ALL HAD OUR FAIR SHARE OF LET-DOWNS AND BRUSH-OFFS, AS YOU'LL SEE...

Vanessa — The first year after I left school was pretty depressing. I went to loads of auditions, but I still had too much free time. I sang every day, I was just a bum at home, singing into my hairbrush in front of the mirror every day. I was still feeling the BRIT School rejection; I was devastated, but I didn't show it. I don't like to show my emotions, so I didn't tell anyone I was upset. 'Whatever,' I said dismissively.

I remember thinking, 'You are going to *have* to do something. You can't just sit at home.' So I got a job in Topshop in Regent Street and that depressed me even more, because I did *not* want to be working in a shop. Still, I had to get some money. I did all right there, but I stopped going after four months. I was running late for work because I'd been held up in a meeting about being in a band, and, although I was often late, this time I was *really* late. Well, they are going to sack me anyway, I thought, so I may as well not go at all.

I'd met Jayne (who went on to become the Saturdays' manager), while I was at Sylvia Young. She is also a casting director and she auditioned me once; she loved what I did and from then on she sent me to auditions. I didn't get anything, though. I *nearly* got stuff, which was hard. One day, I went to a big audition for 'the next Pussycat Dolls'. I didn't want to be in a band like that, but I wanted to sing, so I went along anyway. All the other girls there were six foot, skinny and beautiful dancers – the complete opposite of me. I was the shortest person there. 'Oh my God, I want to die right now,' I thought. 'Why am I here?'

I was better suited to *Daddy Cool*, a West End musical. I went to the auditions and got right down to the final. I really wanted to be in it; I learned the whole script. At the last minute, however, they said that they'd decided to keep the original cast because they were going to do a European tour. It was so frustrating!

I did another audition for a girl group. There were some important people from the US there and they loved my singing audition, but I didn't fit in with the group. Still, one of the guys really liked me and my voice, and arranged for me to go into the studio. He's very nice and he looks after Gaga now. But that didn't work out. It was just another thing that didn't work.

Frankie — S Club Juniors, or S Club 8, as it had become, disbanded when I was sixteen. I knew it was coming for about a year before it actually happened and, as much as I loved it, I was probably ready for a change. I had been caught up in the S Club bubble from the ages of twelve to sixteen. You do a lot of growing up and changing in that time. Still, I remember crying about it with my mum. It was the one thing that really upset me. Touring is just such fun, so I'm glad that it's a major part of being in the Saturdays. Performing in front of thousands of people who have bought tickets to see you and hear your music is the best feeling. I love it so much.

○—

I have no regrets about being in S Club Juniors, but I suppose the one downside was that, when it finished, my friends had all drifted away and established their own groups of friends at school, so I didn't have my own circle of mates outside of the band. Luckily, I had my best friend, Matt, though. Our mums met when they were pregnant in hospital with us, so I'd known him for ever.

○—

I decided that I needed to get my GCSEs, so I paid for myself to go to a private cramming school in London for a year. It was a totally new experience for me to get the Tube, travel in on my own and meet other kids.

○—

Three weeks into term, I was called in to our management office and told that a duet I'd sung with my S Club Juniors' bandmate, Calvin, in the TV drama *I Dream* was going to be released as a single, so I left school and worked on the single. Afterwards, I was signed to my own development deal with 19 Management for about a year. It was amazing. I couldn't believe it.

○—

Yet I always had the feeling that it wasn't really going to work out, even on the day that I signed my contract. It didn't help that I didn't know what I wanted to do, or what direction I wanted to follow. I just didn't feel ready to be on my own at the time.

> # I HAVE NO REGRETS ABOUT BEING IN S CLUB JUNIORS, BUT I SUPPOSE THE ONE DOWNSIDE WAS THAT, WHEN IT FINISHED, MY FRIENDS HAD ALL DRIFTED AWAY AND ESTABLISHED THEIR OWN GROUPS OF FRIENDS AT SCHOOL.
> FRANKIE

It was all quite confusing. From a very young age I had been told what to do and now I was being asked to make my own decisions. 'Which direction do you want to go in?' 'What kind of music are you into?' I didn't know! I didn't have enough experience to know. I hadn't been hanging out with friends, listening to music and developing my own tastes. Unfortunately, I didn't really like any of the songs they gave me. If anything, I veered towards guitar music and I don't think they wanted me to go that way.

○—

After about a year, the whole thing kind of faded out. I felt a bit lost for a while. Since I didn't really have a group of friends, I bummed around at home in Upminster and didn't go out much. I had a boyfriend who I'd been with since I was fourteen, but, although he was lovely, he was no substitute for a group of mates.

Once I got used to the fact I wasn't in the band any more, I started to go out and meet more people. I went through my 'little dark stage', as our manager at the time, Jayne, called it, my brief emo phase. It was during that time that I began to discover my own taste in clothes and music. I also made some really good friends, so I started to feel a lot better.

○—

My best friend, Matt, was the one who got things going. He was still at school at the time and he used to hang out with two girls called Charlotte and Chloe. Knowing that I didn't have any other friends, as sad at it sounds, one day he said to them,

— 'Why don't you come out to dinner with me and Frankie?' We went to our local Pizza Express and I got on really, really well with them. Charlotte went on to become one of my best friends.

Slowly my circle began to expand to include some of my older sister's friends and other family friends. Still, my group of friends remained small, partly through choice.

○—

I think I've always been good in social situations, but I was very self-conscious and didn't like people to ask me loads of questions about being in S Club Juniors. It wasn't that I didn't want to talk about it or that I was embarrassed about it, but I could always tell when somebody was only interested in being friends with 'the girl from S Club Juniors'. That's partly why I don't choose to have a massive group of friends. I have my friends, who I would

> ### AFTER A WHILE, I STARTED THINKING ABOUT GOING BACK INTO THE MUSIC INDUSTRY. I HAD A MANAGER WHO LOOKED AFTER ME FOR A WHILE, BUT THEN HE DISAPPEARED. DON'T QUITE KNOW WHAT HAPPENED THERE!
> FRANKIE

tell everything to and then I have my mates, who probably don't know as much.

○—

After a while, I started thinking about going back into the music industry. I had a manager who looked after me for a while, but then he disappeared. I don't quite know what happened there! I went to America briefly and worked with a singing teacher who took me under her wing, but that didn't work out, either.

○—

Eventually, I got myself a job in a bar where I knew the manager. I really liked working there, except when the customers recognised me. People can be very bitchy and some of them made it obvious that they were pleased to be served by someone who had been in a relatively successful band. I found it a bit embarrassing, but most of the time I loved the job. It was a novelty to be doing something normal. My next job was as a shop assistant in the All Saints section of House of Fraser at Lakeside Shopping Centre, near where I live. It was the most boring thing I've ever done because the shop was tiny and no one ever came into it. I just stood around all day separating hangers and checking the sizes. The only part of the job I liked was stock-checking, because it meant that I could go out the back and scan everything with a scan-gun. I love doing things like that! Also, it kept me out of the front of the shop,

where I felt pretty useless because I hadn't learned how to use the till.
— 'Why can't I pay you for it?' people used to ask.
— 'Sorry, I can't use the till,' I'd say, wincing apologetically.

⚬

By now, I had spent everything I'd made with S Club Juniors. It was weird to go from being paid a lot of money in the band to getting £40 at the end of the week. I remember thinking, 'That won't last me a week!' I was used to having money, so it was a bit of an adjustment. I'm not saying that I'd been rich, but obviously I had no outgoings as a child, so any money I'd earned was mine.

⚬

I had saved a bit over the years, but I wasn't as careful with my money as I could have been and it soon went when I stopped earning. I bought a car and spent money on going out and on everyday expenses, so it went quickly. I don't regret it. I was young and I had fun. As long as I save now and I'm more careful (although I'm terrible at saving! Only money, though!), it doesn't matter.

⚬

After a couple of months, I was desperate to quit, but it was just before Christmas and I felt too guilty about leaving at the busiest time of year, so I waited until after Christmas to make my escape.

Rochelle — When I finished with S Club Juniors, I landed a presenting job on a CBBC programme called *Smile* on Sunday mornings. I did it every weekend for two years, which was really good for me. It was a brilliant experience, but, after it finished, nothing else came up for a good couple of years. So then I did promotional work, which brought me down to earth with a bump. Still, I'm very much a realist, so I would always go out and work if I needed to. I didn't have to pay for food or rent because I was living at home, but I had to pay my phone bill and my car insurance and stuff like that, so I needed to earn money. It's probably the

best thing I ever did because I appreciate this job so much as a result.

◡

At one point, I handed out leaflets for my local radio station. I hated it, mainly because it's totally soul-destroying when you hold out a leaflet to someone and get ignored. Sometimes I used to cheat and chuck the leaflets in the bin! To this day, if anyone hands me a leaflet in the street, I will always take it, even if only to throw it away a few metres along the road. It's worth the bother because it makes such a huge difference to the leafleter.

◡

When I went back on the audition circuit, I had forgotten how ruthless it was. Everybody is competing against each other and sometimes girls can be evil! They'll practically pull each other's hair out to get the part. It's like a conveyor belt and everyone comes and goes very quickly, so it's no place to make friends.

◡

I used to go to as many castings as I could fit in each day, in the hope that I might get at least one. That's the way it works. I was going for every kind of job, from modelling to presenting. To be honest, I was just trying to pay the bills.

Una — First, I went to a music shop and bought my own PA system. Then I called up and visited all the venues that put on live music. I was my own manager and my own roadie, with a car that had folding seats so that I could put my gear in.

ᴍ

Sometimes my parents would drive me. They were great back-up roadies. I did two or three gigs a week. It wasn't a career, but I was making as much money as I would in a normal job at that age and it was good experience. I used to rehearse every single day for hours on end, picking the best cover songs and compiling my set list.

ᴍ

People were always coming up to me and asking for a particular song, so I was constantly expanding my repertoire of favourites from the sixties, seventies and eighties up to the present. I did my own up-

> **I HAD MOMENTS WHEN I THOUGHT ABOUT GIVING UP, WHEN I THOUGHT, 'IT'S JUST TOO HARD; IT'S JUST NOT GOING TO HAPPEN.'**
> UNA

tempo versions of the songs and people often used to dance, even though it was just me on the guitar. Then I'd say,
— 'This is one of my own,' and they'd really take notice.

ᴍ

I gigged all over the country for a few years and developed my confidence as a performer. You can't be shy in this business. You have to be a strong character and have very thick skin. It's no good caring about what people are thinking, even if they're laughing at you. I believed in myself; luckily, my friends and family believed in me as well.

ᴍ

I auditioned for Ireland's equivalent of *Pop Idol* and *The X Factor*. I didn't get very far, but I made it on TV a couple of times and people started to recognise me: 'Hey, you're the girl on that show!' I also did some modelling and extra work in TV soaps, just milling around in the background. Meanwhile, I did a lot of songwriting workshops. Then, in 2004 and 2006, I won the Glinsk Song Contest, the longest-running song contest in Ireland. That was encouraging, and such an honour to win.

ᴍ

In 2006, I was a backing singer for Brian Kennedy in the Eurovision Song Contest in Athens. That was a huge deal for me. Even though I wasn't front of stage, it gave me a taste of performing to a huge crowd and I loved it. There were eighteen thousand in the arena and a billion people watching on TV. I definitely want to do this! I thought. It was such a good feeling.

ᴍ

There were failures along with the successes, though. Still, I kept trying; you have to keep trying. I wrote loads of songs about the pain and hardship

YOU HAVE TO BE A STRONG CHARACTER AND HAVE VERY
THICK SKIN. I BELIEVED IN MYSELF; LUCKILY, MY FRIENDS AND
FAMILY BELIEVED IN ME AS WELL.
UNA

of it: 'When is it going to come, and why is it taking so long?' The carrot was always dangling, but I never managed to grab it. So many people made promises and let me down. I had moments when I thought about giving up, when I thought, 'It's just too hard; it's just not going to happen.' But my friends and family believed in me and kept me going. There was so much encouragement around me.
They would sit me down and say,
— 'Listen, your day will come. You are too good to give it up.'

Then I'd suddenly get a phone call from somebody saying, 'There's a really good gig coming up,' or, 'This person wants to meet you,' or, 'There's a showcase.' I would instantly get excited again. The carrot was always there.

THERE WERE FAILURES ALONG WITH THE SUCCESSES, THOUGH. I ENTERED SONGS FOR OTHER COMPETITIONS AND GOT NOWHERE. STILL, I KEPT TRYING; YOU HAVE TO KEEP TRYING. I WROTE LOADS OF SONGS ABOUT THE PAIN AND HARDSHIP OF IT...
UNA

Mollie — I found school quite hard. I discovered, when I was about eight, that I was dyslexic with a very short-term memory, so reading and revision took me ten times longer than anyone else – but this just made me a harder worker! I was just so determined to do well and I drove teachers round the bend, asking them questions!

∞

But finally, at sixteen, my parents allowed me to go to my first audition, as long as I promised to stay at school until I was eighteen. So on my sixteenth birthday I waked down the road to the newsagents and bought a copy of *The Stage* and made my first phone call. I was lucky that I got into the first band I auditioned for, which was very exciting at the time but it didn't get anywhere, so I concentrated on my school work and, to my amazement, got three As for my A-levels. This led to me getting a place at Lougborough University, and, to my friends and family, my future was sorted!

∞

However, I had different ideas – I had always watched *The X Factor* on TV and so decided to give it a shot! I got through the first two rounds with the producers and then it was time to face the judges! I was absolutely devastated when Sharon Osbourne hated what I was wearing and got the wrong impression of me from it. I couldn't believe she was dashing my dreams because of what I had on. I went outside and, egged on by Ben Shepherd,

> # I HAD ALWAYS WATCHED THE X FACTOR ON TV AND SO DECIDED TO GIVE IT A SHOT! I GOT THROUGH THE FIRST TWO ROUNDS WITH THE PRODUCERS AND THEN IT WAS TIME TO FACE THE JUDGES!
> MOLLIE

> # THERE WERE FOUR OF US – FALLEN ANGELZ – AND WE DID EVERYTHING OURSELVES, FROM CHOREOGRAPHY TO THE STYLING, ARRANGING LOTS OF GIGS AND SONGWRITING. IT WAS GREAT FUN AND WE DID REALLY QUITE WELL.
> MOLLIE

changed into my jeans and T-shirt and went back in and sang a Christina Aguilera ballad. They were then really lovely and said I should come back next year when I was a bit older.

∞

It was shown on TV and from that I got into a band being put together by a girl who was to become one of my best friends. There were four of us – Fallen Angelz – and we did everything ourselves, from choreography to the styling, arranging lots of gigs and songwriting. It was great fun and we did really quite well and even got to the final of boot camp on *The X Factor*.

∞

Just after that, I got a message on my MySpace page from a Jordan from Fascination, head-hunting for a girl. He had seen Fallen Angelz gigging and wanted me to audition for a new girl band he was putting together! I had become quite worldly wise with these kind of things, so I looked him up and sure enough it was genuine.

∞

I couldn't believe it, it was all I'd ever wanted, but my loyalties were to my band mates!
— 'Thank you but I'm already in a band,' I replied. 'I can't leave the girls.'
— 'Please just come and do the audition,' he pressed.
— 'No,' I said, and that was the end of that.

THE SATURDAYS
THAT SATURDAY FEELING

SUMMER 2007. IT WAS JUST ANOTHER AUDITION, OR WAS IT? HAD SOMETHING DIFFERENT FINALLY COME ALONG? WE ALL HAD OUR REASONS FOR BEING WARY AND WE WERE PREPARED FOR ANOTHER DISAPPOINTMENT, YET SOMETHING DREW US TOGETHER. WAS IT FATE, CHANCE OR SIMPLY A CLEVER CASTING DIRECTOR AND A VERY YOUNG TALENT SCOUT?

Rochelle — This was the first project that came up that I really wanted to do. Until then, I took every audition with a pinch of salt and, if I didn't get the job, I wasn't too bothered. When I went up for the Saturdays, even though I'd already been to five auditions that week, I was thinking, 'Oh my God, please!'

Una — I was doing well in Ireland. I had plenty going on and had made quite a name for myself; people knew who I was. Through my MySpace page I'd attracted quite a lot of followers and attention, made contacts and found work. There was lots happening, but at the same time I didn't know where I was heading and felt a bit lost. I needed to get something definite going on. A lot of people told me that my music would go down well in America, but how would I get it heard there?
♔

In the summer of 2007, my mother, my uncle Declan and my Aunt Biddy went to Lourdes, a town in France that attracts millions of visitors a year because it's reputed to be a site of miracles and healing. I've heard that it is a lovely place to meditate or pray. Maybe it's a coincidence what happened next, or maybe my mum's prayers were answered while she was there.
♔

My father couldn't go because he was very busy, so it was just him and me at home.

SUDDENLY, I SAW SOMETHING THAT SAID, 'MAJOR RECORD LABEL LOOKING FOR GIRL SINGERS BETWEEN THE AGES OF EIGHTEEN AND TWENTY-EIGHT.' MY HEART LEAPED. I WAS TWENTY-FIVE.
UNA

THE FIRST AUDITION WAS AT THE SPICE OF LIFE PUB IN SOHO AT MIDDAY. I WALKED IN THINKING, 'THIS IS A BIT RANDOM, NOW. IT ISN'T THE REAL DEAL AT ALL.' I JOINED A QUEUE OF GIRLS.

UNA

— 'Daddy, I think I want to go out of the country,' I told him. 'Although I really want to go to America, I'm going to try London because it's more accessible and it might be easier to get to auditions.'
— 'All right,' he said. 'Perhaps you should do some research on the computer and see if there's anything you can apply for now.' I Googled 'looking for Irish girl singer' and then 'auditions in London for girl singer'.

Suddenly, I saw something that said, 'Major record label looking for girl singers between the ages of eighteen and twenty-eight.' My heart leaped. I was twenty-five. This was my chance to perform in front of a major record label, something I had never done before! I called the number listed.
— 'Are you still looking for people for the band?'
— 'Yes. Can you send us your CD, a CV and biog?'
— 'OK, if you go on my MySpace, you'll find everything there,' I said.

A couple of days later, they called back.
— 'We're really interested in meeting you. Can you fly over next week?'
— 'Yessss!'
The first audition was at the Spice of Life pub in Soho at midday. I walked in thinking, 'This is a bit random, now. It isn't the real deal at all.' I joined a queue of girls. Two girls behind me was someone who looked exactly like Sienna Miller, but I didn't speak to her.

I showed my pictures to the two people there: Jayne, and Jordan Jay, the UK's youngest A&R, who was only twenty-one at the time. The A&R (which stands for 'artists and repertoire') is responsible for spotting talent and overseeing the recording process. I was petrified.

Jane is a casting agent, so she has to be ruthless and she looks a bit scary.
— 'Sing!' she said. I sang a verse and chorus of KT Tunstall's 'Black Horse and the Cherry Tree'.
— 'Fine. Yup, come back next time,' Jayne said.
That was that. I got back on the plane to Ireland and didn't think much more about it.

AT THE FIRST AUDITION FOR THE SATURDAYS, I WAS MORE NERVOUS THAT SOMEBODY WOULD SEE ME.

MOLLIE

Mollie — Six months after Jordan had invited me to a girl-band audition, he messaged me again on MySpace.
— 'I know you didn't want to come to the last audition, but this one really is right up your street,' he said. 'You are exactly what we are looking for. Please just come to one audition. If you don't like the sound of the project, you don't need to take it any further.'

By now, things weren't looking good for Fallen Angelz. At the start, there had been quite a lot of hope and interest, but after *The X Factor*, we were all a bit downhearted. I couldn't stop thinking about the message Jordan had written me and in the end decided to go along to the audition, just to see where it would take me.

THE SATURDAYS 'ISSUES'

DIR: PETRO

CAM: DENIS CROSSAN

Una says that she remembers me from the first audition, but I was in my own little bubble and so nervous that I didn't really notice anyone! I knew if it was for Universal, then it was a big deal – it would definitely be my biggest chance ever!

As I walked in, Jordan gave me the thumbs-up, as if to say 'Good girl for coming,' which was nice. The panel of judges gave nothing away as I sang my heart out, trying to give it everything I had, and, as they interrupted me half way through, my heart sank, but they just held out a piece of paper and said, — 'OK we need you for a call back' and I squealed and ran out of the room!

Una — I carried on with my gigs in Ireland and then I had a call inviting me to the next audition, 'the major audition, the big one'. It was in a club in Soho, down a little lane, across from some sex shop. There was a stage and theatre seats, and there were hundreds of girls. Oh, no! I thought. I noticed Rochelle first, when Jayne called out some names, 'Rochelle Wiseman?'
— 'Yes, that's me,' Rochelle said.
— 'Oh, I don't have you on the list, but that's OK, darling; it's fine, darling,' she said, in the particular way Jayne talks.

Then I saw the Sienna Miller lookalike again, who was Mollie, of course. 'There's that girl!' I thought. She obviously got through as well. She and Rochelle were the girls who stood out the most for me, out of the hundreds of people there. Rochelle and I were practically standing next to each other. I don't know what it was about us, but we gravitated towards one another and soon got chatting.

At first, we joked about how we weren't dressed like the other girls, who were mostly wearing miniskirts and heels. Rochelle was in a cute little purple T-shirt and purple tracksuit bottoms. I was wearing a Nike top that showed off my sporty toned belly. I retained the sporty physique I developed through years of training in the pool.

I overheard someone saying, 'They're not looking for the next Pussycat Dolls; they're looking for the girl-next-door type – nice girls.'
'Well, thank goodness,' I thought.

> ## THERE WERE GIRLS THERE IN HOT PANTS AND HEELS, WITH THEIR HAIR AND MAKE-UP TOTALLY DONE
> ROCHELLE

Mollie and I had to sing two Rihanna songs, 'Umbrella' and 'Unfaithful'. Then we had to dance to another of her songs, 'Breakin' Dishes'. 'Oh, no, dancing is my weakness,' I thought. I was used to hiding behind my guitar, and even though I'd done quite a lot of movement as a child, I didn't feel confident in that area.

A lot of the other girls there were brilliant professional dancers who could do back-flips and other amazing moves, so I couldn't take myself seriously. I thought, I'm going to be kicked out in the first round, but it doesn't really matter. I didn't feel it was for me when I saw how many talented dancers there were. I kept messing up the routine.

Rochelle — I had food poisoning that day and I wasn't going to go. Then my mum said, 'I've got a feeling about this one.' I'm really close to Mum and I always listen to what she says, so I went. Unfortunately, it was really bad food poisoning and I was in the toilet vomiting between every song and dance.

I felt really underdressed too. There were girls there in hot pants and heels, with their hair and make-up totally done, whereas I wore a tracksuit and trainers because I was there to dance, and my hair was tied up. I stuck out like a sore thumb. I should have made more of an effort, I thought. But I'd been out of the audition process for so long . . .

Jayne later said, 'We wanted to see you, not a made-up you,' so it turns out that I did the right thing, but at the time it made me very nervous.

I was still feeling really ill when we were asked to sing a Rihanna track, either 'Umbrella' or 'Unfaithful'. I chose 'Unfaithful' because it's a ballad and I thought I'd be able to show my voice off better.

Well, I was shockingly bad; it was even worse than my dancing. 'Thanks,' Jayne said to the girl who had gone before me. Then she looked at me. Certain that she was going to say 'no' to me, I just wanted to leave. I was so embarrassed.
Instead she said,
— 'Come back after lunch. Make sure you learn that dance.'
— 'OK, I will!'
Una came up.
— 'What did she say to you?' she asked.
—'She said to come back after lunch and learn the dance,' I said.
— 'She said the same thing to me!'

So Una and I snuck off together. We didn't eat lunch. We spent the whole time in the corner, like two geeks, two keenos, practising the dance. It was really hard and neither of us could do it. Even Jayne agrees that we didn't get it right after all that. We tried our best, though, and that's what counts.

> I HADN'T BEEN TO ANY DANCE CLASSES EITHER, SO I FELT SCARED.
> ROCHELLE

I was nervous throughout the audition. I'd been used to dancing with the Juniors, but it was made easy for us and our dances mainly involved simple hand moves. Either way, I'd had two years off from it and was out of practice. I hadn't been to any dance classes either, so I felt scared. Whether you've got rhythm or not, however good you are, you look like you can't dance when you're in a room full of trained dancers.

I didn't see Mollie until the end of that day, when I thought, Sienna Miller has turned up to a girl-band audition! I was really convinced it was her, until I spoke to her later!

Una — Rochelle and I swapped numbers. 'If you hear anything, call me,' we said. We kept in touch after that.

Rochelle — We clicked straight away and swapped numbers without knowing if we were going to get through or not. It's very unusual to make that sort of connection at an audition. It's a bit of a cliché, but we were just drawn to each other.

Mollie — Then came the dance audition. I *love* dancing but I never had lessons as a child. But the girls in Fallen Angelz taught me loads – they had all had years of experience and they were always happy to show me over and over until I got it right! When I arrived, I had never seen so many pairs of leggings and leg warmers and fancy dance shoes. It was so intimidating! I went up to Una, because she looked friendly, unlike some of the other girls, who looked really scary.
— 'Do you know the dance routine?' I asked her.

WE SPENT
THE WHOLE
LUNCH TIME
IN THE CORNER,
LIKE TWO GEEKS,
TWO KEENOS,
PRACTISING
THE DANCE.
IT WAS REALLY
HARD AND
NEITHER OF
US COULD
DO IT.
ROCHELLE

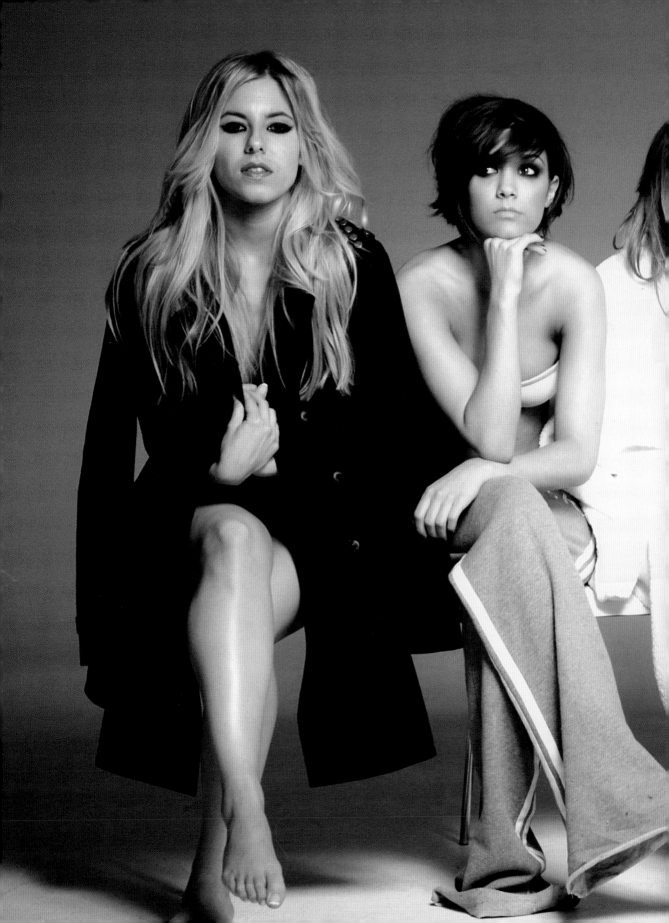

— 'I know bits of it,' she said. It was the same for me; I had picked up parts of it, but I was struggling with the rest. It was impossibly hard.

— 'Where are your jeans from?' I asked, and that was it – we clicked.

∽

I didn't stop practising for a second, and at one point I went outside and practised using a shop window as a mirror. I didn't care about being stared at by very surprised passers-by – this was my chance and I was determined not to blow it!

∽

They called my name and in I went. I have no idea how well I did the routine but it must have been OK, though then suddenly Jayne, who was a very scary member of the judging panel, shouted out,

— 'OK girls – freestyle.' I thought to myself, 'Oh gosh! What does Britney do?' And off I went – dancing my socks off! Then someone said,

— 'OK girls – these ones are through,' and they called my name! I was just sighing with relief when

Jayne shouted out to me,

— 'Excuse me!' I stiffened slightly.

— 'Oh no . . .'

— 'Is there anything you can change into?' she asked. I looked down at the baggy tracksuit I was wearing, which to be fair did look like something from the Bronx next to everyone else's dance gear! 'Yes,' I replied because luckily at the last minute I had slipped a denim skirt into my bag for afterwards. I went off to change, and when I came back in for the next round, Jayne said with a smile,

— 'Oh, that's a lot better. Thank you.'

Una — I felt much more comfortable singing. After all the Rihanna stuff, we were allowed to freestyle and sing what we wanted. I rocked out 'Sweet Child o' Mine' and then sang Jeff Buckley's 'Hallelujah', which hadn't been covered to death back then. I sang it *a cappella* and I think that's what impressed the judges.

♕

I was the first to be called by the panel. I had no idea that I was sitting down in front of our future management, our future label head and potential writers and producers. The panel consisted of Brian Higgins and Miranda Cooper (Xenomania), Colin Barlow, Peter Loraine and Jordan Jay (Polydor), David Massey (Universal America) and Jayne Collins, the casting agent.

— 'We really like your style,' they said. 'We like the fact that you are a songwriter, you play guitar, and you're not the typical girl-band type. We definitely feel you bring something to the band.'

Bring something to the band? I thought. Am I in the band now?

— 'We admire your dedication, and it's great that you have so much experience,' they went on. 'But is this what you want – as a solo singer-songwriter?

— 'Do you really want to be part of a band?' asked Peter.'

— 'I want to do music,' I replied earnestly. 'I want to perform. I have a passion for it and I'm here for that reason, so of course I would love to be in the band.' David gave me his card and said to call if I didn't get into the band.

While I was on the plane home that night, Jayne called. 'They love you!' she said. 'You've got to come back for the final audition. There are seven girls in the running now, so you must be stronger and more determined than ever. Show them how much you want it.' That's when I started to take it all seriously.

Mollie — Twelve of us were left after the second audition. In the evening, we had to stand up and sing in front of each other. That's when I saw Rochelle for the first time. I remember thinking that she was really good. I was sure I recognised her from somewhere, but I didn't know where.

Rochelle sang amazingly. Then Una got up and sang and she was amazing as well. I was one of the last to be called, by which time my heart was beating so hard it was about to jump out of my chest. I was incredibly nervous, but I managed to get through a Fallen Angelz song. Afterwards, Jordan said to me, 'If you get asked to sing again, don't sing a song nobody knows. People like to hear a song they know.' I felt panicked that I'd done the wrong thing, but thought that it was too late to do anything about it.

You always watch the people you think are going to get through and so I found myself watching Rochelle. She was just so bubbly, chatting away to all the other auditionees. She didn't seem at all nervous. I was also watching Una. Like me, she was quieter. We kept ourselves to ourselves a bit more.

I was really happy when I heard I had got through to the final audition, but my excitement was tinged with sadness. It was a bittersweet experience because I was so worried that if I got in I would have to leave my Fallen Angelz friends. We four girls had the same dream and had worked so hard together; I had also been the youngest by far and they had all looked out for me. I would miss them and I felt like I would be letting them down! Yet this opportunity was everything I'd ever dreamt of.

Getting to the final stage was a bit of a double-edged sword, but I was still over the moon to have made it!

A LOT
OF THE OTHER
GIRLS THERE
WERE BRILLIANT
PROFESSIONAL
DANCERS
WHO COULD
DO BACK-FLIPS
AND OTHER
AMAZING MOVES,
SO I COULDN'T
TAKE MYSELF
SERIOUSLY.
UNA

FRANKIE SANDFORD

FOR FIVE GIRLS, WE'RE QUITE CALM, REALLY. OF COURSE, WE HAVE OUR MOMENTS. WE ARE PICTURED OUT A LOT, BUT THAT'S ONLY BECAUSE WE KNOW MORE PEOPLE AND GET INVITED TO MORE THINGS NOW – AND IT DOESN'T MEAN THAT WE'RE PLASTERED EVERY TIME WE GO OUT!

```
AGE    —   21
BIRTH  —   14 FEBRUARY 1989
SIGN   —   CAPRICORN
FROM   —   UPMINSTER
```

How do you boost your confidence when you're feeling low? — Occasionally I wake up and think everything looks horrible and my hair isn't right. Every girl wakes up to one of those days every now and then, don't they? I just deal with it. If I'm having one of those days, I put on something that I know I feel comfortable in, like jeans and a vest. For us Saturdays, those days when you're not feeling your best can be terrible because we still have to put on our tiny little stage outfits! Because of that, I think I've got used to just getting on with it. Being around my friends helps me feel better.

Flirting tips? — The girls always say to me,
— 'Did you fancy that guy you were talking to?'
— 'No, I was only talking to him!' That's just the way I am, the way I act, I'm quite tactile, but I won't give someone loads of compliments; I'm more likely to take the mick out of them!

If a guy comes up to me and tells me I'm beautiful, my defences instantly go up and I'll brush him off. I'm not interested. If he comes up to me and takes the mick out of me, I'm more likely to laugh and think it's funny and engage him in conversation. I like that banter. If someone hasn't got that, then I'm not really interested. If I say something and he gets offended, I think, 'Oh dear, he wouldn't cope being out with me and my mates!'

If I liked someone from afar, I'd catch his eye as if I didn't mean to. I'd look at him and then not look again. I'm not a game-player or anything, though. If I like someone, I will let him know I like him, but at first I let him know that he should come and talk to me if he wants to! I'm always completely myself and I'm not embarrassed to be me. I don't care if I've got an Essex accent. I don't care if I like music someone else doesn't like. I'll find something funny in that. I'm quite honest. Although I flirt,

I ALWAYS GET A LITTLE BIT MISCHIEVOUS WHEN I'M BORED. ONE DAY, WHEN THE RECEPTIONIST WASN'T THERE, WE WENT OFF AND STUCK DOWN EVERYTHING ON HIS DESK WITH SELLOTAPE, INCLUDING THE PHONE.

I'M NOT A GAME-PLAYER OR ANYTHING, THOUGH. IF I LIKE SOMEONE, I WILL LET HIM KNOW I LIKE HIM, BUT AT FIRST I LET HIM KNOW THAT HE SHOULD COME AND TALK TO ME IF HE WANTS TO! I'M ALWAYS COMPLETELY MYSELF AND I'M NOT EMBARRASSED TO BE ME.

---

a guy knows if I really like him or not. Actually, I find it easier to flirt and mess around with a guy if I don't really fancy him. If I like him, I'm still playful, but I'm not going to put my guard up and act like I don't like him. I'm not one of those people who waits twenty minutes to text back, so that he thinks I'm busier than I am. I wouldn't blow a guy out just to keep him interested. I'd say, 'OK, let's go out, then.'

I can laugh at myself, which I imagine is quite nice for guys, who may be just as worried as you are that they're going to say the wrong thing. I always say what I probably shouldn't.

A while ago, someone took me out to a restaurant I don't like. He had already booked it, so I didn't say anything because I felt bad. Once we were there, looking at the menu, he said,
— 'What do you want? This is great, isn't it?'
— 'Actually, I don't really like this restaurant,' I replied. 'There's not a lot on the menu I like.'
— 'What! I can't believe you came,' he exclaimed.
— 'I didn't want to say anything, but I didn't want to be dishonest,' I told him.
In the end, I found something I liked and we stayed and had a nice dinner, but that's an example of me just coming out and saying something. Actually, it was probably really annoying.

IF A GUY COMES UP TO ME AND TELLS ME I'M BEAUTIFUL, MY DEFENCES INSTANTLY GO UP AND I'LL BRUSH HIM OFF. I'M NOT INTERESTED. IF HE COMES UP TO ME AND TAKES THE MICK OUT OF ME, I'M MORE LIKELY TO LAUGH AND THINK IT'S FUNNY AND ENGAGE HIM IN CONVERSATION.

Most embarrassing moment:
—
We were learning a dance where we had to be a bit sexy. As I was doing my best Beyoncé strut, my foot slipped from underneath me. Along with all my hotness! I fall over all the time during performances!

Favourite Saturdays single?
—
'Ego,'
—
because I love the song and I really enjoy doing the dance routine that goes with it.

Five words That best describe me:
—
Messy
Mischievous
Caring
Witty
Original

On my iPod:
—
Parachute
Kids in Glass Houses
City and Colour
Kings of Leon
Paramore
Rihanna

Favourite
items in
my wardrobe:
—
My Topshop
Boutique vest tops.
—
Fendi Shoes,
Staple black pair,
my first pair of
expensive shoes.
—
Denim hotpants,
great all year
—
Mango skinnies
I've had them years
and they are still
the best fitting
jeans I own.

Favourite
Saturdays video?
—
'Issues,'
—
because it
reminds
me of a
really exciting
time for
the band.

I CAN LAUGH AT MYSELF, WHICH I IMAGINE IS QUITE NICE FOR GUYS, WHO MAY BE JUST AS WORRIED AS YOU ARE THAT THEY'RE GOING TO SAY THE WRONG THING. I ALWAYS SAY WHAT I PROBABLY SHOULDN'T.

WHAT WOULD I WEAR ON A FIRST DATE?

I ALWAYS LIKE TO LOOK LIKE I HAVEN'T MADE THAT MUCH OF AN EFFORT ON A FIRST DATE. IF I'M REALLY DONE UP, THEN I FEEL LIKE AN IDIOT. SO I WOULD WEAR SOMETHING LIKE A NICE PAIR OF JEANS THAT I FEEL COMFORTABLE IN, A PAIR OF HEELS AND A VEST TOP AND BLAZER.

What would you wear on a first date? — I always like to look like I haven't made that much of an effort on a first date. If I'm really done up, then I feel like an idiot. So I would wear something like a nice pair of jeans that I feel comfortable in, a pair of heels and a vest top and blazer. Nice and dressy, but not in your face.

Would you kiss on a first date? — Never, because I find kissing such a big deal and I get so nervous! I can't cope with it, and also I think, 'Why should I? I don't even know you yet!' If I wanted to, then I would, but I never do. I just like to give them a peck on the cheek and keep them guessing!

Favourite word? — 'Awesome.' I say it a lot!

On going out — For five girls, we're quite calm, really. Of course, we have our moments. We are pictured out a lot, but that's only because we know more people and get invited to more things now – and it doesn't mean that we're plastered every time we go out!

I never used to like going out, but now I do. We've made some friends within the industry, people like JLS, Pixie Lott, Chipmunk and Taio Cruz. There's a circle of us who often go to the same gigs and we've ended up getting to know each other. I wouldn't necessarily ring them up and say, 'Do you want to do this?' but it's nice to go to a party that everyone else has been invited to, especially as we're all around the same age.

WE'VE MADE SOME FRIENDS WITHIN THE INDUSTRY, PEOPLE LIKE JLS, PIXIE LOTT, CHIPMUNK AND TAIO CRUZ.

THE SATURDAYS
MOVING CLOSER

THE NEARER YOU GET, THE MORE NERVE-WRACKING IT BECOMES! IT WAS TIME TO STRETCH OURSELVES, SING BETTER, DANCE BETTER AND SHINE. OTHERWISE, IT WAS BACK TO SQUARE ONE ON THE AUDITION CIRCUIT. SOME OF US FELT WE WERE IN WITH A CHANCE, BUT WERE WE? AND WHERE ON EARTH WERE FRANKIE AND VANESSA?

Rochelle — Surprisingly, I was called back. I don't know why! They left me stewing for a few weeks before I heard anything, so I thought I hadn't got through. In the meantime, I went to other castings and got a few modelling bits and pieces. At the next audition, we were told,
— 'Please don't do any other auditions now.'
That sounded like good news to me and I began psyching myself up, thinking, 'Maybe I've got it!'
— 'Nothing is definite yet,' Jayne added, 'but you are doing well. We'd rather you didn't go to other castings because we don't know when we might need you to come for another day.'

'Wait a minute!' I thought. 'I've still got to earn myself some money.' On the other hand, I really wanted it . . . 'OK, fine!'

For the next audition, I invited Una to come and stay. I didn't know this girl at all and yet I drove to Stansted Airport and picked her up. We dropped her bags at my house and I said,

— 'Do you want to go out for dinner?' We went for a Chinese at some random dodgy joint near me.

The next day, we drove to the studio together. Again it was very odd because we just got on so well. We had a subconscious understanding of one another, I think, and we get on just as well now as we did then. It's a bit spooky, really!

We instantly clicked. I didn't know the others at all at this stage. I had no idea that Frankie was going to be in the band, so it was a relief to know that at least Una and I got on really well.

Mollie — For the next round, we went into the studio with Brian Higgins, who writes for Girls Aloud. It was an amazing day, because Brian Higgins' house is like a mansion and his studio is just how you imagine a studio to be. Getting there was slightly chaotic, though. There was torrential rain and all the Tubes were flooded, so everyone was running late.

FOR THE NEXT ROUND, WE WENT INTO THE STUDIO WITH BRIAN HIGGINS, WHO WRITES FOR GIRLS ALOUD. IT WAS AN AMAZING DAY!
MOLLIE

We each went in individually to record chunks and verses of various songs. Brian gave me really positive feedback, so I came away feeling good. There were seven of us in the running now. Frankie and Vanessa had been invited at this stage but I didn't see any of the others. Frankie has since told me that she saw me sitting outside the studio, but ran past me because she felt too nervous to talk to anyone!

Frankie — I was on a week's holiday with my friend Charlotte when I heard about the auditions for the Saturdays. It was the worst holiday I've ever been on, in Zante, one of the Greek islands. We booked it at the last minute and chose it because the hotel looked all right, but we obviously didn't check it out properly, because it turned out to be a total disaster! It was one of those places full of Brits on holiday, people getting drunk and beating each other up. It was horrible. To make things worse, on the day we left to go on holiday, I woke up with a stomach bug and was ill for the next four days. I could barely eat and I couldn't drink! Although I'm not a massive drinker, it would have been nice to have a glass or two on holiday, but I was just too ill. I lived off nothing but Rich Tea biscuits.

Towards the end of the week, I felt well enough to go to the beach. One day while I was in the sea, my phone started ringing and I got out just in time to pick it up. It was Peter Loraine from Polydor.
— 'We're starting a new girl-band project,' he said. 'Just wondering if you'd like to come down for a chat?'

Part of me thought, 'Good, something has come up at last!' But another part of me felt a bit disappointed. 'Oh, another band,' I thought. Having already been in one pop group, it hadn't occurred to me that anybody would want me for another. I had assumed that I'd do something different. I also felt a bit nervous about the idea of a girl band because most of my friends are boys. Anyway, I was contemplating going to university by this stage.

All my friends were applying and I'd rung up and found out that I could get in as an adult, going on experience instead of exam results. My plan was to do music management, which I probably would have hated, thinking about it now!

When I got back from holiday, I went along to Polydor to find out more. That's when I discovered that Rochelle had gone for the auditions and was probably going to be selected for the group. 'That's really weird!' I gasped. We still kept in touch every couple of months, but hadn't spoken for a while. I phoned her as soon as I left the meeting. 'I had no idea you were going up for it!' I said. 'Wouldn't it be strange if we both got it?' I was really pleased that somebody I knew might be a part of the project. It made it less daunting.

> # I WAS BRIGHT ORANGE AT THE TIME, BECAUSE I HADN'T LEARNED MY LESSON ABOUT USING FAKE TAN, WHICH I REALLY DON'T NEED.
> FRANKIE

I joined the audition process at the final stage, when there were seven of us left. We were filmed singing and dancing together; we also practised doing pieces to camera, saying things like, 'Hi. My name's Frankie.' I was bright orange at the time, because I hadn't learned my lesson about using fake tan, which I really don't need. Plus, my hair was short and blonde, because I was going through a stage of cutting it and dyeing it different colours. I have no idea why they wanted me there – I looked a right state!

Vanessa — After all the rejections I'd been through, I kind of gave up for a while and started saving up to go on holiday with a friend. The week we were heading off, Jayne called me again.

WHEN I DISCOVERED THAT ROCHELLE WAS PROBABLY GOING TO BE SELECTED FOR THE GROUP TOO, I WAS REALLY PLEASED THAT SOMEBODY I KNEW MIGHT BE PART OF THE PROJECT. IT MADE IT LESS DAUNTING.

FRANKIE

VANESSA

— 'Listen, there's another audition for a girl band. I think you should come because it's going to be a big deal.'

— 'I've heard this before,' I replied. 'You said that about the other one. Well, I'm not going to cancel my holiday.'

— 'You have to!' she insisted, but I wouldn't change my mind. 'Right, OK,' she said, 'we'll just have to film you singing.'

A couple of days later, we met up in the studio and she filmed me singing 'Umbrella', which I hated. I mean, I love the song, but I would have preferred to sing something that I could belt out.

When I got back from holiday, I was called for a dancing audition. There were seven of us; I had done dancing at school, every Thursday and Friday, whether I liked it or not and I wasn't an amazing dancer, but I knew the basics.

Looking around at the others, I felt I was getting somewhere and realised that I really wanted to make it into the band. But I was expecting things to turn out just as they always did — nearly getting it but not quite — so I tried not to get excited. I had learned my lesson after the disappointment of the *Daddy Cool* auditions.

Mollie — The next audition was at Pineapple Studios. We were sent an email saying,

— 'OK, girls, the next audition is a dance audition, so bring some heels.'

'You must be joking!' I thought. I had almost never worn a pair of heels in my life. I'm such a flat-shoe person. Knowing it would be disastrous if I tried to dance in heels, I decided not to take any. The last thing I wanted was to look ridiculous. I knew I wasn't a good enough dancer

to carry it off.

I'm such a late person that I made a supreme effort to be early and actually arrived first. Vanessa was the second person to arrive. Since I hadn't seen her before, I wondered if it meant that they were bringing loads of new people in.

— 'Hi. How are you?' I said, going on to confess that I was nervous because I hadn't had any dance training.

— 'Don't worry,' she said. 'I'm not very good, either. I'm more of a singer than a dancer.'

Although that was partly true, I think she was saying it just to make me feel better, because I later found out she had been at stage school and was a great dancer. I liked her immediately and thought she was absolutely stunning. Then Frankie walked in. I hadn't seen her before, either!

When all seven of us had arrived, Jayne said,

— 'OK, put your heels on.'

— 'Sorry, I forgot mine,' I said.

She was really angry and huffed a bit, but I thought, 'Trust me, you don't want to see me dancing in heels!' So while everyone else danced in high heels, I was in my trainers.

We lined up for the dance routine, which was set to the track that we had recorded with Brian Higgins. I was put next to Frankie, who was very friendly and chatty. She was wearing massive heels. 'How can she dance in those?' I wondered. I didn't know then that even if you put Frankie on stilts, she could dance in them. She is that good!

Next we each had to speak into a video camera, one at a time. We were told to say a few things about ourselves and then the clips would be shown to everybody at Universal. I hadn't prepared

I KNEW MOLLIE WOULD BE PICKED, BECAUSE SHE WAS THE ONLY BLONDE. WITH FRANKIE, I THOUGHT, WHO IS THIS BEAUTIFUL, TALENTED BABE, JUST BACK FROM HOLIDAY?

UNA

anything to say, so I just blurted something out about having a dog called Holly, that I lived I lived in Surbiton and I loved Britney. It was complete rubbish. When you're as nervous as I was, you can't really control what's coming out of your mouth. You've probably noticed that about me by now!

Una — Oh, no, it was dancing again! By now, at least they knew that my strength was my voice, but I gave it all I had. The other girls were so much better, but never mind. Jayne still has the audition tapes and they're so funny, but I have asked her never to show them to anyone. I didn't go into the audition too nervous and I think that stood me in good stead. I didn't feel sick or anything and I thought 'If this is meant to be, it will be.'

I knew Mollie would be picked because she was stunning and had a great voice. With Frankie, I thought, 'Who is this beautiful, tanned babe, just back from holiday?' She exuded confidence, especially when it came to her dancing.

I thought she seemed perfect for the band. Although I hadn't heard her voice, I was sure she would be selected. Rochelle also seemed a dead cert because I knew how brilliant her voice was. Then I heard that Vanessa was a brilliant singer so

> ## 'YOU WILL NEVER GUESS WHO I'M AT THE AUDITION WITH!' I SHRIEKED. 'TWO OF THE S CLUB JUNIORS!'
> MOLLIE

I thought, she's in, plus she was beautiful. Funnily enough, I was unsure if I would get on with Vanessa. She was very quiet and we didn't get chatting, so I wasn't sure if she liked me or not. But now I'm probably closest to her and more comfortable with her than with anyone. She's the youngest in the band and I'm the oldest, but we

have a real connection. I can't remember an awful lot about the other two. I think one of them said that she had been spotted on the street. She was a beautiful, tall, model type who had been tapped on the shoulder a couple of weeks before and asked along to a girl-band audition. No disrespect to her, but I had wanted it so much all my life and worked so hard and had the talent! It would have been heartbreaking if she had got in and I hadn't. She and the other girl were great, though. I often wonder what they think now when they see us on TV.

Mollie — That was the final round, so we thought, and we all went out for dinner to Wagamama afterwards. I got on with Una straight away.
— 'I bet you'll get in the band,' she said, as we were walking to the restaurant.
— 'Why do you think that?' I asked.
— 'Because you are the only blonde one left! They always have a blonde one.' I looked around at the others, and realised that she was right, so I really hoped that it would increase my chances.

At Wagamama, I went into the toilets with Frankie and we talked about how much we wanted to be in the band. From what she was saying, I gathered that she and Rochelle knew each other.
— 'How do you know each other?' I asked.
— 'We were in a band together.'
— 'A band!' I said.
— 'S Club Juniors,' she said.
'Well, when I heard that, I became a bit star-struck, because they'd been in such a successful band already!' Immediately after the meal, I phoned my sisters.
— 'You will never guess who I'm at the audition with!' I shrieked. 'Two of the S Club Juniors!' I thought it was so cool. If I told the girls that now, they'd think I was really sad, but I was just so excited at the time. I always take photos of everything, so I said, 'Let's take a photo, in case some of us do get in the band. It would be really good to look back on.' I asked the waiter to take it, but I can't find that stupid photo now. I don't

know where it is. I am still exactly the same: I take photos of everything. The girls are always saying, — 'Oh, Mollie, it's like having the blooming paparazzi around!'

Rochelle — A week or so later, the call finally came.
— 'OK, we want you to come in for a meeting.'
'This is really dragging,' I thought. 'Are they going to go for it or not? Are they actually going to put a band together? What's going to happen?'

Mollie — A few of us exchanged numbers and in the days to come we texted each other saying, 'Have you heard anything?' We knew that if we didn't hear anything, then it was a no. They don't call you to tell you that you haven't got it.
∞

Nobody heard anything for a while, and then finally they called us each up to say,
— 'Can you come into Universal for the last round?'
∞

I immediately texted the others.
— Yes! I've been called in!
— Me too!
Weirdly, the two I hadn't exchanged numbers with hadn't been called.
∞

My mum came with me this time. Some of us were early and waited in a café outside Universal. Frankie and Rochelle, my mum and I sat there wondering what would happen in this next round.
— 'We are so close now. Cross your fingers, girls!'
Vanessa and Una arrived last and we were called up to the head of Polydor's office, although we didn't know he was the head at this point. The five of us sat down, and I remember thinking, 'I wonder if they are testing out how we look as a five? Perhaps they're going to call three of us back and test us with the other two.'

Rochelle — Colin Barlow, the co-president of Polydor at the time listed all the things that the band was going to do, including release an album, bring out a perfume, write a book (!) and support Girls

Aloud on the Tangled Up Tour. 'This is really good news for whoever the band is,' I thought. Then I said,
— 'Excuse me, who is in the band? Are we the band? Nobody has told us what is going on.'
Colin Barlow started laughing his head off.
— 'You girls are in the band. Why do you think I'm telling you all this stuff?' All of a sudden, we were screaming,
— 'Oh my God, we're together now!'

> 'YOU GIRLS ARE IN THE BAND. WHY DO YOU THINK I'M TELLING YOU ALL THIS STUFF?' ALL OF A SUDDEN, WE WERE SCREAMING, 'OH MY GOD, WE'RE TOGETHER NOW!'
> ROCHELLE

Mollie — Nobody had told us! 'Wow, we have actually done it!' we shouted, as we jumped up and hugged each other. Nothing else that was said after that sank in for me. I sat there in a daze of happiness.
∞

When I walked out of the building, I expected fireworks to go off, trumpets to start blasting, and a band to play, but everything was exactly the same as it had been an hour earlier. I wanted to scream to everybody in the street, 'AHHHHH!'
∞

I was so glad my mum was waiting outside. I ran to the car, got in and shouted, 'I've done it!' We both burst into tears. 'I can't believe this,' I sobbed. 'I've wanted this since I was six years old and now I've actually got it!' Yet I felt so sad, at the same time, because it meant that I was going to have to say goodbye to the Fallen Angelz.
∞

It took ages to pluck up the courage to call the girls and tell them that I was leaving. But, as it turned out, they were really happy for me. That shows what great friends they were. It could have gone completely the other way, which I would have understood. I still to this day speak to them all the time. They come to our gigs and I always get them tickets.

Frankie — After being unsure about whether I wanted to be in another band, once I knew more about the project and had met the other girls, I was really hungry for it. Now I'd had a fresh taste of performing, of being back in the industry, I realised that was where I truly wanted to be. Especially because they made us wait and wait before we signed the contract.
— 'I really want to do it now!' I told my mum.

Vanessa — Everything was moving so slowly. 'Come on!' I thought. 'I really want this to happen.' We did some recording here and there, but we wanted to be busy.
— 'We want to be doing something every single day,' we told Jayne.
— 'We don't want days off. We just want to work.'
— 'You won't be saying that in a year's time!' she said, laughing. She was right. A year later, I was pleading with her,
— 'When are we going to have a day off?'

Mollie — The Saturdays' audition process had gone on for about eight weeks through July and August, but it wasn't until January that we actually signed the contract. The five of us were calling each other non-stop. 'Have you heard from the management? Have you heard from the label?'
∞
At one point, we hadn't heard anything for weeks and we started to worry that the whole thing might be a wind-up. Was it actually going to happen?

I kept calling Frankie and Rochelle because they knew how the industry worked, but all they could say was, 'It's a bit weird.'
∞
I can never sit around and do nothing, so I did some modelling at the Abercrombie store in Central London for a few months. Every day I hoped that the phone would ring and someone would say,
— 'Are you ready to get going?'

Una — It just seemed so far away, as if it was never really going to happen, but it did happen in the end. After flying in from Ireland for five auditions and paying my own way on a tight budget, I kept having to fly over for recording sessions and dance classes at my own expense.
∞

As soon as we signed the deal, I had a call to say, 'You need to move over here now, because it's going to be full steam ahead.' So I moved to North London immediately. Being on my own in another country initially made me feel a bit older than some of the girls, but that didn't last. When you are in the same boat, going on the same journey, it is irrelevant how old you are. We were all in exactly the same place in our lives, regardless of age.
∞

It was hard because I didn't have any family and friends in England, apart from my boyfriend at the time, who moved over with me. He was an actor pursuing his career in London. However, shortly afterwards he received an opportunity which meant moving to LA, so we went our separate ways. We were given an advance on our royalties, so I was able to afford to pay my rent for a year, and we were given a very basic wage to live off. I had a bit saved up, but there was no time to earn anything else on the side. The band was everything now.

WHEN YOU ARE
IN THE SAME
BOAT, GOING
ON THE SAME
JOURNEY, IT IS
IRRELEVANT HOW
OLD YOU ARE.
WE WERE ALL
IN EXACTLY THE
SAME PLACE
IN OUR LIVES,
REGARDLESS
OF AGE.
UNA

THE SATURDAYS
MAKING FRIENDS

WHAT HAPPENS WHEN YOU TAKE FIVE VERY DIFFERENT GIRLS AND PUT THEM TOGETHER 24/7? IT COULD GO EITHER WAY, COULDN'T IT? ACTUALLY, IT COULD GO QUITE A FEW WAYS! UNDERSTANDABLY, WE WERE ALL A BIT ANXIOUS ABOUT WHETHER WE WOULD GET ON. WHAT IF WE DIDN'T REALLY LIKE EACH OTHER? WOULD WE HAVE TO PRETEND?

Mollie — Just before we signed the deal, we were flown to Norway to record some songs for our first album. We were told we would be staying in a suite. 'We are so showbiz!' we said to each other, expecting it to be like P. Diddy's suite.

We arrived to find that we were squashed into a double room with two hotel beds and three camp beds. 'Wait, this isn't the pop-star lifestyle we were expecting!' we said, falling about laughing. Being in such close proximity was great for bonding, though. We quickly learned a lot about each other.

I got on well with the girls, but being away with four virtual strangers was nerve-wracking.

> WE REALISED THAT WE WERE ALL THERE FOR DIFFERENT REASONS, EACH BRINGING SOMETHING INDIVIDUAL.
> MOLLIE

We didn't know each other at all and I hadn't been away from home very much. I felt self-conscious having to sing in front of them, especially Vanessa. She has one of the most amazing voices I've ever heard and every time she sang I thought, 'What am I doing here?' But, as time went on, we realised that we were all there for different reasons, each bringing something individual to the band.

I like to go to sleep quite early and so does Rochelle, whereas Una and Vanessa are night owls. They don't go to sleep until about two o'clock in the morning. But I was used to waking up at 7 a.m. and I really suffer and get a bit tearful if I don't get enough sleep. We chatted non-stop the first night. We were so excited and there was so much to find out about each other! As the evening wore on, I started to feel tired, but didn't want to seem unsociable. I struggled to stay awake. Then Rochelle zonked out on one of the sofa beds. 'Thank God somebody else is tired!' I thought. To be honest, I was tired for the whole trip because I was constantly trying to keep up.

Everybody was still asleep when I woke up on the first morning. I thought, 'I'm not going to miss out on breakfast!' So I quietly slung on my tracksuit and crept downstairs to the dining room. They were still asleep when I got back to the room, so I slipped into bed and went off to sleep again. The next time I woke up, everyone was complaining,

— 'I'm really hungry!'

— 'I'm not,' I said smugly. 'I've had a full breakfast!'

Rochelle — Mollie and I always share a room now, even if we don't need to. If I have my own room, I'll go and find Mollie and watch TV with her. We like being really girly together and we go to bed much earlier than Vanessa, Frankie and Una. The only problem with sharing with Mollie is that the girl makes me late and I have to scream at her.

I've developed a strategy for making her early, which is to tell her it's later than it really is. So, if we're due somewhere at eight o'clock, I tell her that we've got to be there at a quarter past seven, and we get out of the door at five to eight, so you can imagine how late we would be if I didn't do it! Unfortunately, she has recently cottoned on, so it doesn't work any more!

Frankie — The Norway trip was our first opportunity to spend proper time together. We slept next to each other, squashed up like sardines, so it's lucky that we got on well. In fact, being in each other's pockets helped us get to know each other really quickly. I was nervous, but straight away I knew that the girls were fine and I soon became really comfortable with them. When you spend so much time together, you pick up on each other very quickly.

No one came with us – no management, no one – so it was quite scary, just going out to Norway to meet these people who we didn't know. It was particularly weird for Rochelle and me, because we were used to having chaperones in the S Club Juniors' days, but now we were alone.

It was my eighteenth birthday while we were there. I remember thinking, 'Oh, it's my birthday!' We didn't do anything special; I couldn't be bothered.

We had been working really hard in the studio, so we just went to bed because we were so tired! Still, just being there was special, and when I got back home, I went out with my friends to celebrate.

One day, we had our picture taken together and somehow it ended up on the Internet. No one was supposed to have seen us yet and we all look awful in it! Mollie had bunches and stripy trousers, and I was wearing a big baggy jumper. It was a disaster at the time, but it's quite nice to look at it now and see how far we have come. We all look so funny.

Vanessa — In the beginning, I was very shy, so I don't think any of the girls realised what a loudmouth I really am. I'd say, 'Hi. All right?' and then I'd be so scared to say anything else that I'd look away or start rummaging through my bag. They are lovely girls, though, and so it wasn't long before we started getting on. We clicked and I began coming out of my shell, which seemed to surprise them. 'We didn't think you were going to be like this!' they said.

> ## I WAS NERVOUS, BUT I BECAME REALLY COMFORTABLE WITH THE GIRLS STRAIGHT AWAY.
> FRANKIE

Frankie — Vanessa was very quiet and timid at first; she never said a word. Then when she got to know us, she was so blooming loud! She has the biggest laugh and she's a bit nutty. Sometimes Vanessa and I can be quite mischievous together. We get bored easily, especially when we're waiting around at the studio. One day, when the receptionist wasn't there, we went off and stuck down everything on his desk with Sellotape, including the phone. I always get a little bit mischievous when I'm bored. That's when my sense of humour comes out.

Rochelle — I loved Vanessa from the moment I met her. People think she's shy, but she's not shy at all! She doesn't like mornings. You won't hear a peep out of her. We'll all be in the car and someone will say, 'Is everyone here?' It sometimes feels like one of us is missing because Vanessa is at the back, hiding beneath her scarf and shades.

Mollie — Vanessa sometimes drifts off into her own little world. You can be talking to her for twenty minutes and suddenly she will say, 'Sorry, what was that?' and it becomes clear that she hasn't been listening to a word you've been saying. At other times she can be a complete motormouth.

Vanessa — I'm a free spirit and I live in the moment. I get up, look at the schedule and get on with whatever we're doing. I never think about next week. My catchphrase is, 'Sorry, what are we doing tomorrow?' I do things spontaneously, depending on how I feel on the day, whereas someone like Mollie thinks things through for about a year before she actually does them. We are very different, but we connect!

Frankie — It's hilarious to think about the difference between how Mollie was when we first met her and how she is now. She didn't have a clue about make-up: she had one Maybelline cover-up stick and that was about it. Her hair was always down and unstyled. She wore Ugg boots most of the time because she couldn't walk in heels. She was just one of those people who looked effortlessly, naturally pretty. Now, though, she's really into her cosmetics, she backcombs her hair, and she loves wearing heels, even though she always makes a fuss about not being able to walk in them! Once, when we were in the studio, she whipped out some Femfresh wipes. Rochelle and I looked

at her, thinking, 'What's she going to do with those?' When she started cleaning her armpits with them, we said,
— 'Mollie, what are you doing?' We hadn't known each other long and so didn't know that Mollie is obsessed with making sure she doesn't smell.
— 'Just cleaning my armpits,' she said.
— 'With Femfresh wipes? Mollie, they are for women's bits!'
— 'No, they are just for women,' she replied.
— 'They're not, Mollie!'
— 'Oh my God,' she squealed. It turned out that she had been using them for years as wipes. She had even bought a pack of them when she was out shopping with a boy. To this day, I laugh about it. It's the funniest thing.

Mollie — I've learned so much! In the beginning, although I loved clothes and shopping for high street fashion, I'd never heard of Balenciaga or Christian Louboutin. Thank goodness for Rochelle! I'd never bought a magazine in my life, apart from pop magazines with Britney in. The girls couldn't believe it when I told them. 'But why would I buy magazines?' I said. They all laughed. Unlike Rochelle and Frankie, who were working and earning from a young age, I had never been able to afford a Chanel bag or anything like that, so my knowledge of designers was very limited.

> MOLLIE IS VERY UPBEAT BUT, LIKE ME, SHE WORRIES A LOT, ABOUT ANYTHING AND EVERYTHING. IT WAS WORSE AT THE BEGINNING, BECAUSE NONE OF US FELT SECURE.
> FRANKIE

I'VE LEARNED SO MUCH! IN THE BEGINNING, I KNEW NOTHING ABOUT MAKE-UP OR FASHION BECAUSE I'D NEVER BOUGHT A MAGAZINE IN MY LIFE, APART FROM POP MAGAZINES WITH BRITNEY IN.

MOLLIE

NO ONE WAS LEFT OUT OR FELT LIKE AN OUTSIDER. THERE WAS NONE OF THAT. YOU MIGHT THINK THAT BECAUSE TWO OF THE GIRLS HAD ALREADY BEEN IN A BAND TOGETHER, THEN THEY MUST HAVE THIS REALLY COOL FRIENDSHIP, BUT FRANKIE AND ROCHELLE CAME INTO THE BAND SEEING IT AS A FRESH START, JUST LIKE THE REST OF US. WE ALL GOT ON REALLY WELL.

UNA

I was using a Maybelline concealer as a foundation because I didn't understand the difference between a concealer and a foundation. I dotted it around my face and rubbed it in. Maybelline, Vaseline and mascara were all I knew.

∞

A few months down the line, I overheard the girls talking about make-up.
— 'Do you wear Chanel or Estée Lauder?' they asked me.
— 'Just Maybelline,' I said. I got out my concealer stick to show them.
— 'You do realise that's concealer, don't you?' they said. I had no idea!

∞

These days, I wouldn't go out with a caked face because I like to keep my make-up quite natural, but I love to learn about it. I'm really interested in fashion too and I'm always reading magazines. I haven't bought a Chanel handbag yet, but I did buy a Balenciaga! I was more interested in buying my car, though – a Nissan Figaro. It's nothing fancy, a bit like a Noddy car, but I've always wanted one.

Frankie — I was always into make-up, even before S Club Juniors. I was one of those girls who thought a lot about my clothes, had my hair done and wore heels every day. Even when I was twelve, I wore cowboy boots (because my mum wouldn't let me wear high heels). I wanted Spice Girls' wedges, but I wasn't allowed the high ones, just the lame, really

low ones. I was always into looking glamorous, whereas now I'm more laid-back and I sometimes wear flats.

○—

It's good that we're all such individuals. I was into different music when we got together, but the others didn't dismiss it; they were interested in hearing it, even though they said, 'Oh, no, why do you like that?' For a while, I was obsessed with Agyness Deyn, but none of them got it. (I don't get it any more, either!) It's good to have different opinions. You always find common ground as well.

○—

I quickly bonded with Mollie because we are both worriers, although we are quite positive too. Mollie is very upbeat but, like me, she worries a lot, about anything and everything. It was worse at the beginning, when the band first came together, because none of us felt secure. If I couldn't sing something or get something right, I was anxious that I might be dropped. From early on we'd ring each other and say,
— 'Have you done this? I can't do it.'
— 'Me neither,' the other would say.
We soon learned to egg each other on and encourage each other, because neither of us wants the other to feel like that. We understand what it's like to be a worrier.

○—

Now, if I can't do something, I just go on trying until I can. If that doesn't seem like it's working out, then I'll find another solution.

IT'S GOOD
THAT WE'RE
ALL SUCH
INDIVIDUALS.
I WAS INTO
DIFFERENT
MUSIC WHEN
WE GOT
TOGETHER,
BUT THE OTHERS
DIDN'T DISMISS
IT; THEY WERE
INTERESTED . . .
FRANKIE

Mollie — I'm very much a good girl through and through. I don't drink, so I was hoping the others weren't too wild! I haven't found a drink I like yet, but even if I did I don't think I'd go overboard. I have a fear of being out of control.

There were some pretty wild times with the ski team when I was younger – those guys work hard and play hard – but I always wanted to be in control of myself. It never holds me back though; I'm always first on and last off the dance floor and I love to party – I just don't need alcohol to have a good time.

I'm used to being the youngest: I've got two older sisters and I was skiing with older people all of my childhood. I was one of the youngest in my class at school and I was the youngest in Fallen Angelz. So it felt weird when I found out that I was the second oldest in the Saturdays. My immediate thought was I hope they don't look up to me for advice! But, as it happens, they are all pretty worldly wise and I actually feel like one of the youngest!

Una — The girls are really funny and I just love people who make me laugh. They're not up themselves in any way, so within no time we were all just taking the mick and laughing at each other. 'Thank God I'm with decent people here,' I thought. They make me feel really comfortable.

No one was left out or felt like an outsider. There was none of that. You might think that because two of the girls had already been in a band together, then they must have this really cool friendship, but Frankie and Rochelle came into the band seeing it as a fresh start, just like the rest of us. We all got on really well.

Frankie — My nan always calls me 'sunshine and showers' because I'm one of those people who can be really chatty and sociable one day and then another day I'll want to keep myself to myself. I enjoy my own space. I have done since I was little, when I could happily play on my own in the garden

for hours. I don't need to have company or be entertained, and I was hoping the others would understand that. Being with other people continually can be hard.

> I REMEMBER THINKING RIGHT AT THE BEGINNING THAT UNA AND I WERE QUITE SIMILAR AND I SUSPECTED THAT SHE WAS PROBABLY NERVOUS AS WELL.
> MOLLIE

Now that the girls know me well, if I'm a bit quiet one day, nobody thinks, 'What's wrong with her?' If there is something wrong, I'll say so. I'm open and upfront about my feelings. I don't know where I get it from, because I don't come from the sort of family where we talk about our feelings. Although, to be fair, we don't avoid it either.

These days, I know when one of the girls is in a bad mood or upset. I know how to handle it, whereas at the beginning it took a little while to figure it out. If I'm in a bad mood, I like to be left on my own, but one of the others might need to be made to laugh. So you figure that out with your friends as time goes on and I think it's something we've all done really well.

Rochelle — Frankie's nan got it right: Frankie is either bubbly or quiet. She's never horrible, but you can't be sure what mood she will be in when you see her. There is nothing wrong with her when she's in a silent mood; that's just how she is.

I always got on well with Frankie. The only reason we lost touch was because we wanted to concentrate on our own friends when we left S Club Juniors, having been together almost every day for four years. We kept in touch, though; we spoke now and again, to catch up.

Una is either really, really happy or she's quiet. I get on so well with her. We all do stuff together out of work, but I genuinely feel that Una is my big sister. She's got a fantastic personality, although she can be quite fiery. If someone has done something really wrong, I won't send Una to talk to them. I'll talk to them instead, because I can quietly reason with them, whereas Una will explode and rage at them, then regret it afterwards. She doesn't really mean it, so I say, 'Una, leave it. I'll do it.'

Mollie — I remember thinking right at the beginning that Una and I were quite similar and I suspected that she was probably nervous as well. We would look out for each other and talk on the phone a lot to see how we were finding everything.

She was back and forth from Ireland, which I imagine must have made things even more scary. At least I could go home to my mum every night. I didn't like the thought of her staying in a hotel by herself, so she sometimes came and stayed at mine.

> ## ROCHELLE IS FUNNY, QUITE LOUD AND CONFIDENT.
> FRANKIE

Vanessa — Una and I get on very well. We were rebels together, especially in the beginning. I seek her out when I feel I want to party. We egg each other on; we're the naughty twins.

As time went on, it became obvious that Rochelle was the best organiser. She's the one who says, — 'Come on, girls, we need to get going!'

Frankie — Una was very sweet and laid-back. I always thought it was a bit harder for her as she had to move over from Ireland to be in the band. She played guitar and was already a singer-songwriter, so I thought she was really talented. It was quite nice for me to have Rochelle there, because I knew her so well. I think the others liked having us there because they didn't know how things worked in the beginning, whereas we had more of an idea. So they knew that if we were worrying about something, it was something to worry about, and if we weren't, then everything was OK.

Rochelle is funny, quite loud and confident. She's also a real tidy freak. She knows what she likes and she likes her labels! As time has passed, she has come to be seen as the mum of the group.

Mollie — My first impression of Rochelle hasn't changed much. Chat, chat, chat! I'm usually a complete chatterbox as well, but I was so nervous at first that I wasn't my normal self. So it was good being around Rochelle who'd make me laugh and I latched on to her a bit. We were soon to discover that we had the same sense of humour and so Mochelle was born!

Rochelle — We were quite scared on that trip to Norway because we still hadn't signed our contract and we felt we were being tested. 'Are they planning to chuck one of us out?' we wondered. It was impossible not to feel insecure.

We're so lucky that we got on well from the start – and still do. Obviously everyone has their off-days and sometimes we tell each other to shut up. We're also very honest with each other. I've been known to come to work and say, — 'Girls, it's that time of the month and I'm not

feeling good. Just leave me alone. Don't direct any jokes at me because I will cry.'

We really have a very sisterly relationship, which I'm so grateful for. We were lucky in the Juniors too, but I didn't get on with them as well as I do with these girls. We didn't have that closeness. It's such a good thing.

Mollie — I loved our music from the start. It was just up my street – perfect. After all, I could have found myself in a girl band that was all about sex, drugs and rock and roll, which would not have been my thing at all. Instead I was with girls I had a lot in common with and the music was the kind of thing I would have on my iPod. In fact, the girls laugh at me because I sometimes put on our albums, but I like the songs!

Una — I was pleased that quite a few of the producers we worked with complimented me on my voice. They also expressed surprise that I've got a rock-country style within a pop band, because it's quite unusual. Mine's a mongrel voice, the product of all my musical influences. They like it because I'm not your stereotypical pop singer, although I can do R&B riffs and everything else.

It was full steam ahead once we had signed our deal. We went straight back into the studio to finish our first album. Our label had already found the best songs possible for us. Everything had been planned, from the music to our image. We barely had a day off for the next year and a half.

Frankie — We quickly realised that we all have our roles in the band – not in a defined way, but we all play a part and we're just as important as each other. I know I can't do the ad-libs in a song, so it doesn't bother me that Nessa does them all, because she is amazing and makes the song sound better. Una has a husky voice, so she'll sound amazing on another part. In the studio, I'll say, 'Una should do that part,' and she will do the same for me.

I tend to sing higher and I'm always a bit nervous about singing low, but the other day in the studio, Una said,
— 'No, go in and do it low. You'll sound good. Go on.'
— 'No, no,' I said, because I didn't feel confident enough.
— 'Go on, do it!' So I did it and it sounded amazing! That's how things work with us. Mollie and Rochelle, all of us have strong and unique voices that bring something different to the band. We all want everyone to do their best and play a part in each song and video, because each of us knows how it feels to be missed out. We understand and we want the music to be the best it can be, so if Mollie is good at something and they want her to do it, fine. Let her do it, because it will help us all. We are best friends working together.

Una — It surprises people to hear that we get on so well. It's funny, I know I would have hung around with the girls at school if we'd been in the same class. Even at the auditions, I gravitated towards them. Now what we have is a little bit stronger than just being friends. We're a work family, like sisters, and very protective of each other. If somebody said anything about one of them, I'd take it personally.

We don't argue. We genuinely don't. We get a bit irritated with each other every now and then, but it's not personal. I love that about us and I think that people will always remember us for being such good friends. We haven't got a bad word to say about each other.

> IT WAS FULL STEAM AHEAD ONCE WE HAD SIGNED OUR DEAL. WE WENT STRAIGHT BACK INTO THE STUDIO TO FINISH OUR FIRST ALBUM. OUR LABEL HAD ALREADY FOUND THE BEST SONGS POSSIBLE FOR US.
> UNA

MOLLIE KING

> *Fortes fortuna iuvat – fortune favours the brave! I have that engraved on the back of my iPod!*

SMILEY AND PROBABLY IRRITATINGLY ALWAYS UPBEAT, I SEE THE GOOD SIDE OF EVERYTHING AND EVERYONE. A HOPELESS ROMANTIC, I'M A FAMILY GIRL, LOYAL AND TRUSTWORTHY AND PEOPLE TEND TO TELL ME ALL THEIR SECRETS! I WOULDN'T EVER BETRAY SOMEONE'S TRUST AND I HOPE I'M A GOOD LISTENER. BUT I'M ALSO VERY AMBITIOUS AND DRIVEN AND THERE WAS NO STOPPING ME ONCE I KNEW I WANTED TO BE A POP SINGER.

```
AGE   — 23
BIRTH — 4 JUNE 1987
SIGN  — GEMINI
FROM  — SURREY
```

On my iPod — Apart from the Saturdays (sorry, but I genuinely really like the songs!), there's Britney, Michael Jackson, Paolo Nutini, John Mayer, Regina Spektor and *High School Musical* (1, 2 and 3). I love pop like Britney, but I also love acoustic guitar: I have everything by Britney, of course. As a performer, she is still one of the best and I love her music, although I think her old tracks are probably my favourites. I feel for her because I think she is going through a tough time. I just love her. I am so biased. I won't hear a bad word said about her!

Worst fashion disaster? — When we wore matching outfits that looked like bin liners to the *High School Musical* première! I was fancying my chances with Zac Efron, but there was no chance in that outfit! We looked dreadful. Vanessa Hudgens was there – I love her – as well as Zac Efron. They looked fantastic together. She looked so cool and classy and hot, and we just looked ridiculous. My mum called me the next day and asked,
— 'What were you guys wearing?'
— 'Thanks, Mum,' I said. 'Say it straight!'

Have you ever had your heart broken? — There was a boy I was infatuated with when I was fifteen. He was really sporty, looked like he had just walked off the *Home and Away* set, and we had a lot in common – the only problem was that every time he spoke to me I was just completely lost for words and turned into a nervous wreck! I had a crush on him for what seemed like for ever but at the time it just wasn't reciprocated. Hey ho, you win some, you lose some!

I'M A
COMPLETELY
POSITIVE PERSON.
I JUST SEE GOOD
THINGS AHEAD.
I REALLY WANT
TO GO TO
EUROPE, BACK
TO ASIA AND TO
AMERICA TOO!
I'M DYING TO
SEE MORE OF
THE WORLD.

Favorite items in my wardrobe:

—

Balenciaga handbag
Ray-Bans
Denim jacket
Temperley sunglasses
My Abercrombie jeans

On my iPod

—

Britney Spears
Michael Jackson
Paolo Nutini
High School Musical
John Mayer
Regina Spektor

Favourite Saturdays single?

—

It's very hard to choose, but I'd probably say 'Issues'. I love the lyrics and, whenever we perform it, I always get a feeling inside that reminds me of how lucky I am. When you're singing a ballad, there's more time to look around and think about how fantastic it is to be on stage.

Fashion advice?

—

Wear what suits you. Don't be ruled by a particular fashion if it doesn't suit your body shape! I think I know more or less what looks good and bad on me, so I try to stick with that. I love girly clothes, and I prefer short dresses to long ones.

What do you look for in a boyfriend?

—

I like someone who makes me laugh, is spontaneous and fun! It's important they get on with my family and get the sister approval!... and if I can boss them around that's always a bonus!

Favourite Saturdays video?

—

I love the feel of the 'Issues' video. It was filmed outdoors and we all look natural. I fell in love with the house on the beach in Kent, where it was partly shot.

Five words that best describe me:

—

Craaaazy
Fun
Honest
Smiley
Determined

I COMPLETELY OVERUSE THE WORDS 'AMAZING', AND 'PERFECT'. I ABBREVIATE EVERYTHING AS WELL, SO I'M ALWAYS SAYING 'AMAZE' INSTEAD OF 'AMAZING'.

I LOVE THE RED CARPET. I FEEL LIKE I'M PLAYING A PART, BEING A MOVIE STAR. I'M USUALLY SECRETLY THINKING, 'WHAT AM I DOING UP HERE?' IT IS SO COOL. THE GIRLS JUST HAVE TO STOP ME STARING AT THE CELEBS THOUGH – I DON'T THINK THERE IS ANY HOPE FOR ME, I WILL NEVER STOP BEING STAR-STRUCK!

Are you a good shopper? — Yes, when I don't take a bag with me! My new resolution is to stick my phone and my card in my pockets so that I can shop light. My boyfriend refuses to go shopping with me because I'm so indecisive and it drives him mad! I have to go by myself now.

Red-carpet tips? — I love the red carpet. I feel like I'm playing a part, being a movie star. I'm usually secretly thinking, 'What am I doing up here?' It is so cool. The girls just have to stop me staring at the celebs though – I don't think there is any hope for me, I will never stop being star-struck! I don't pout and I haven't mastered the over-the-shoulder look yet. Una is so good at all that. I asked the girls how to look sexy and they told me to stop smiling and squint! I'll let you know how I get on! . . .

Fashion advice? — Wear what suits you. Don't be ruled by a particular fashion if it doesn't suit your body shape! I think I know more or less what looks good and bad on me, so I try to stick with that. I love girly clothes and I prefer short dresses to long ones. I also love wearing casual clothes. I'm a flat-shoe person through and through. I can't walk in heels. Frankie is giving me lessons – I think she was born in them!

Favourite words? — I completely overuse the words 'amazing' and 'perfect'. I abbreviate everything as well, so I'm always saying 'amaze' instead of 'amazing', for example. Anything that can be abbreviated, I will shorten. When we went to Disneyland in Paris, I started abbreviating the names of the rides. Space Mountain became 'SM'.

— 'SM, anyone?' The girls were like,
— 'Mollie, you are so sad.'
Still, I think 'The Sats' has caught on!

Favourite Saturdays single? — It's very hard to choose, but I'd probably say 'Issues'. I love the lyrics and, whenever we perform it, I always get a feeling inside that reminds me of how lucky I am. When you're singing a ballad, there's more time to look around and think about how fantastic it is to be on stage. When we're busting routines for the faster songs, there's no time to think anything at all!

Favourite Saturdays video? — I love the feel of the 'Issues' video. It was filmed outdoors and we all look natural. I fell in love with the house on the beach in Kent, where it was partly shot. I want to live in it when I'm older! I also like the 'Work' video because it has a completely different feel. I loved our outfits and it was really fun dancing with the dancers at the end.

> I ASKED THE GIRLS HOW TO LOOK SEXY AND THEY TOLD ME TO STOP SMILING AND SQUINT! I'LL LET YOU KNOW HOW I GET ON! . . .

THE SATURDAYS HELLO, WORLD!

THE DEAL WAS DONE, THE CONTRACT WAS SIGNED, AND WE'D RECORDED HALF OF THE ALBUM! NOW IT WAS TIME TO CHOOSE THE DÉBUT SINGLE, MAKE A VIDEO AND LAUNCH THE BAND. WAIT – FIRST WE'D BEEN BOOKED TO DO OUR FIRST EVER LIVE PERFORMANCE AT G-A-Y AND THEN GO ON TOUR WITH GIRLS ALOUD. NO PRESSURE, THEN!

Vanessa — I was petrified before the show at G-A-Y. I hadn't given a big performance since I'd left school – all I'd done was practise in my room – so I had no confidence. I was so nervous that I could barely breathe and so frightened that I couldn't enjoy it. You could see my legs shaking as the curtain came up. I've never been as happy as I was when we came off stage, just because it was over. I did really badly in that performance; I was shocking. When I watch the video back, I feel so embarrassed.

Rochelle — It was the very first time we performed publicly, so it was like a launch of the group: 'Here are the Saturdays!' The pressure was on. We knew we had to be good. It was really exciting and it's always going to be a massive memory. Unfortunately, it was awful. It's funny what nerves can do to you. You usually lose the nerves when you get on stage, but we were all thinking, 'Get me off! Get me off!' We didn't like it at all, and we didn't do very well.

My mum was there and my eighty-year-old nan. Poor Nan! Although my family were in a sectioned-off part of the club, I'm sure Nan was wondering, 'Where am I?' I certainly don't think she knew what 'G-A-Y' stood for. I thought, 'Why have I brought my nan to a sweaty club?' But actually she loved it. After the performance, she and Mum said, — 'You were fantastic!'
Well, my mum thinks that anything I do is great,

so I said,
— 'OK, Mum, I'm not asking you.' I went
up to Jayne and asked, 'What was it like?'
— 'It was good, but it wasn't the best you can do,'
she replied. There was my answer.
— 'OK,' I said. 'I just needed to hear the truth.'

Una — A certain amount of nerves is healthy,
but the intensity of nerves I was experiencing that
night was definitely not healthy! They were horrible;
they consumed me completely. Mollie and I were
the worst, I think. There's a film on YouTube of us
talking about how nervous we were. 'My heart is in
my throat,' Vanessa said. 'I mean my heart is in my
mouth!' We couldn't even talk. I was wearing massive
heels, and I was very unused to wearing heels then.
I'm an Ugg-boots and flip-flops person and I found
it impossible to dance. Obviously, I've learned now!
I've also got used to wearing false eyelashes!

I think we were particularly nervous because
we felt we would be quite carefully scrutinised
by the audience. I was shaking the whole way through

the performance – I don't know how I made it to the
end. I can't imagine ever feeling that nervous again.
I kept thinking, 'Why do I want to put myself through
this?' I should have loved it, but I hated every second
and wanted it to be over as soon as possible.

Vanessa — I was just as scared before our first
show with Girls Aloud, but it was a completely
different experience. Once I was out there, it was
great; my confidence returned and I've never
enjoyed being on stage so much. We all came
off stage buzzing. 'Yeah! Yeah! Yeah!' we shouted
at one another. It was great.

> ONCE I WAS OUT THERE,
> IT WAS GREAT; MY
> CONFIDENCE RETURNED
> AND I'VE NEVER ENJOYED
> BEING ON STAGE
> SO MUCH.
> VANESSA

Frankie — We were told that we'd be going on tour with Girls Aloud right from the start, but we didn't think it would really happen. The next thing we knew, we were on tour with this massive band! We hadn't met the girls properly before, so they seemed quite distant and untouchable. Then suddenly they were sitting opposite us at the dinner table in the canteen. It was awesome, really surreal. Whether you are the support act or not, it's a very big deal to do an arena tour. You couldn't ask for a bigger or better promotion, but we were really thrown in at the deep end. We rehearsed for ages, and took singing and dancing lessons, trying to learn four dance routines. We developed at different stages, so it was a question of getting everybody to be the best they could be, learning to sing together and gelling as a band.

We were all so nervous before the first show that we felt sick, but we had such a good reaction from the audience that the nerves disappeared. Two seconds into our performance, we were all loving it. Everything feels great once you're up on stage. We were buzzing when we came off.

Once we got used to performing on the tour, we became much more critical of ourselves. 'That wasn't a good one!' we'd say when we came off stage. It inspired us to practise more and make sure we did our best every time. It was such a cool experience for us being on tour. Mollie always says that it was the best time she's ever had. Everything was so new and exciting, and you never knew what was going to happen next. It was so much fun.

Vanessa — It was hard for us because the audience didn't know who we were and we had to try and grab their attention and gear them up for Girls Aloud. We didn't have any special effects or an impressive set, just a black curtain behind us, so it wasn't an easy task. It was incredible to get the response that we did. It was a real buzz and felt like a very good sign of things to come. Yes! They actually like us!

Mollie — I can't tell you how good it was going on that tour. It was one of the happiest times of my life. It seems strange to say that, because I had just broken up with my boyfriend of four years, which was very bad timing, but I was so excited that it couldn't have come at a better time, in a way. I was going to be so busy doing what I'd always wanted to do that I wouldn't have time to think about the break-up. It was a whirlwind and I loved it.

> EVERYONE LIKED US!
> IT WAS A RELIEF, BECAUSE
> I THINK A FEW PEOPLE HAD
> ASSUMED WE WERE TRYING
> TO REPLACE OR COMPETE
> WITH GIRLS ALOUD BEFORE
> THEY SAW US, WHICH OF
> COURSE WE WEREN'T.
> UNA

Una — It was brilliant, the best experience ever. I loved performing in all the arenas, getting up on stage in our fluorescent outfits, even though we were singing in front of a black curtain, with about a square foot in which to do our routines. Everyone liked us! It was a relief, because I think a few people had assumed we were trying to replace or compete with Girls Aloud before they saw us, which of course we weren't. Girls Aloud have never interfered with our path and we have never interfered with theirs.

There has never been any kind of rivalry; we're on the same label, Fascination, so we're very friendly. They gave us our start. The first question people ask us is, 'So, how are you different from Girls Aloud?' You may as well ask, 'How are Girls Aloud different from the Spice Girls?' We're just different people with different personalities and different music.

I WAS TOTALLY STAR-STRUCK WHEN I SAW GIRLS ALOUD FOR THE FIRST TIME. WHEN CHERYL AND KIMBERLEY CAME INTO OUR DRESSING ROOM AND WISHED US LUCK, I COULDN'T BELIEVE IT. NORMALLY YOU CAN'T SHUT ME UP BUT, WHEN THEY WALKED IN, MY JAW DROPPED TO THE FLOOR AND I HAD NOTHING TO SAY.

MOLLIE

Frankie — Girls Aloud were really nice, but they were also manically busy. You don't realise until you go on your own tour how much other stuff there is to do. You assume it's just performing the show, but there's all the promotion, press and meeting fans that goes with that, plus the travelling. We used to see them around and we often ate together in the tour canteen, but there wasn't much time to hang out. The first night, Cheryl and Kimberley came into our dressing room to say, 'Hi', while we were doing our hair and make-up.

— 'We remember when we used to do our own hair and make-up,' they said. 'It feels like just yesterday!' That was nice to hear.

Mollie — I was totally star-struck when I saw Girls Aloud for the first time. When Cheryl and Kimberley came into our dressing room and wished us luck, I couldn't believe it. Normally you can't shut me up, but when they walked in, my jaw dropped to the floor and I had nothing to say.

— 'Hey, girls. How are you feeling?' they asked us. They must have thought, 'God, that blonde one is a bit gormless!'

∞

Our first night on stage was just unbelievable. It was everything I'd ever wanted. We weren't a successful pop band yet, but still I was there with Girls Aloud performing to an arena. Before we went on, I said, 'Come on, let's give each other a high-five.' I've always been into the idea of being a team, and now it's stuck and we do high-fives before all our performances. At the start of our set, Rochelle

and I walked on stage from the right and the others came on from the left. I'll never forget standing there with Roch, whispering, 'Good luck!' We were so nervous.

∞

I felt really high when we went on. I was surprised that I couldn't see the audience, though. I'd never been on a massive stage like that before, so I didn't realise that all you can see is black, because the spotlights are so bright. I did a lot of squinting, trying to see people. It was good in a way, though. I had expected to be confronted with thousands of staring faces, which might have affected my confidence.

∞

It didn't go entirely smoothly: at one point, I was giving it all that I had and my mike pack flew out the back of my dress, leaving my headphones swinging about. Then Rochelle's shoe broke. It wasn't perfect, but we had an absolute blast. I kept thinking, I'm up here on the stage that Girls Aloud are going to perform on!

YOU ASSUME IT'S JUST PERFORMING THE SHOW, BUT THERE'S ALL THE PROMOTION, PRESS AND MEETING FANS THAT GOES WITH IT, PLUS THE TRAVELLING.

FRANKIE

We sang four tracks and at the end I didn't want to leave the stage. I wanted it to go on for ever. I waved a frantic goodbye to the crowd, as if they had come to see us, not Girls Aloud. It makes me cringe to think of it now.

When we came off stage, we were just so happy! We jumped on each other and screamed madly. Back in our dressing room, I made everyone stay in their costumes and took a photo. I've got the pictures on my laptop at home; we all looked a bit sweaty and the worse for wear, but you can see that we were totally on a high. Every night it was the same, just unbelievable. Whenever we could, we stayed and watched the Girls Aloud show; they were just amazing. They looked like superstars as they came down from the roof at the start of their show.

It really inspired us watching them.
— 'We've got to up our game' we kept saying to motivate one another. We wanted to be as good as them one day.

Frankie — People think that touring is all about partying, but we would often go straight to bed after a show. We go out a bit more these days, but at the beginning, we were so aware that we didn't want to mess it up that we didn't even think about doing a performance hung-over. We still never go out the night before something important, unless it's someone's birthday. Even then, we would plan it, so it's never before a recording day.

Vanessa — Everyone was well behaved on the Girls Aloud tour, until one night when Una and I decided to have a drink downstairs at our hotel. Just a little chat and one drink. Well, one thing led to another and, almost without realising it, I'd had quite a bit to drink. Big mistake! The next thing I knew Frankie had come down to see what was going on, because someone had told her we were still in the bar. 'Oh my God!' she said, when she saw us. She had to help us get back to the room. I was stumbling up the stairs. It was so embarrassing!

We slept too long the next morning and were horrified to find that we had missed breakfast. We were so hung-over and so hungry that we badly needed food. Finally, we persuaded someone in the kitchen to cook up a massive plate of hash browns and loads of toast. We wolfed it all down, desperate to feel better. I learned my lesson after that. 'Never again!' It's a mistake you only need to make once.

Frankie — It was great when we had the chance to chat to Girls Aloud because they always talked to us on a level that made us feel like we were friends: 'How are you finding this?'; 'If anybody says this to you, then just say that . . .'
— 'Oh God, does this ever happen?' they'd ask.
— 'Yes, what's that all about?' we'd say. Something I'll always remember is when Cheryl told us about a song they really didn't want to do that ended up

IT WAS GREAT
WHEN WE HAD
THE CHANCE TO
CHAT TO GIRLS
ALOUD BECAUSE
THEY ALWAYS
TALKED TO US
ON A LEVEL THAT
MADE US FEEL
LIKE WE WERE
FRIENDS.
FRANKIE

being one of their biggest hits. I think it was 'Love Machine'. The girls told their label,
— 'We hate it! We don't want to do it.'
The label said, 'No, you are going to do it.' They were all really pissed off and then it went on to be a huge hit.
— 'Sometimes you just have to listen,' Cheryl told us. 'No matter how much you don't want to do something, you might have to swallow your words.'

Rochelle — I thought we would see more of Girls Aloud, but I know what it's like now, because we didn't really see our support act on our tour. You have a job to do and you have to get on with it. There are a million and one things to do when you're headlining.

When we did see them, they were so lovely. We saw them in catering all of the time and they often came and ate with us. We exchanged general chit-chat, just day-to-day stuff. They certainly didn't give us loads of advice. They are just nice girls and they put on an amazing, inspirational show. We went to all their end-of-show parties.

> WE SHOT OUR FIRST VIDEO, FOR OUR DÉBUT SINGLE, 'IF THIS IS LOVE', AND EVERYTHING BECAME EVEN MORE EXCITING.
> ROCHELLE

After our set, when we went to watch their performance, we turned to each other and said, 'Wow, this is what we need to be doing.' They were a big act and so they had the money to put on a massive show. I remember being blown away by the stage effects and choreography.

Vanessa — I used to think, 'Wow! I want to be like them.' They are lovely and watching them gave us so much inspiration. It made me want to get to that level so badly. They were amazing and looked like they were having loads of fun. We didn't watch the

> WE WERE RIGHT AT THE BEGINNING OF EVERYTHING, WHICH MEANT THAT THERE WASN'T MUCH PRESSURE ON US AND WE COULD JUST HAVE FUN.
> FRANKIE

show every night, because sometimes there weren't enough seats for us. We could have watched from the wings, but we didn't want to be in the way; it would have been really annoying while they were doing their quick changes between songs. We stayed to watch them as often as we could, though. I couldn't get enough of their show; I could easily have watched every single one.

Frankie — We were right at the beginning of everything and no one really knew us, which meant that there wasn't much pressure on us and we could just have fun. It also meant that we were touring on a tight budget. Our stage costumes went in a suitcase at the end of every show and never got cleaned, so they stank by the end of tour!

Rochelle — We loved every minute of being on that tour, so we didn't even think about being tired. Then we shot our first video, for our début single, 'If This Is Love', and everything became even more exciting. It was just before we performed at the O2. It felt different shooting a video now I was older. I really loved it. There were tears on that day, though. Mollie didn't like her make-up, and Vanessa wasn't happy with the way she looked, either. When it's your first video, you just want it to be perfect. Of course, you don't need to freak out about it. All you need to do is go up to the make-up artist and say, 'I want to change my make-up.' When the pressure is on, though, it's easy to get upset and it was quite difficult on that occasion because, unfortunately, the make-up artist on that shoot didn't speak

English very well, so I had to go through her assistant. Still, everyone was happy in the end.

When you see a description of the plan for a video shoot, you visualise in your head how everything is going to be, including how you are going to look, so it can throw you if it isn't as you imagined. Not that it's ever bad; it's just not how you imagined it. With five girls, it's likely that at least one of us is going to cry. I didn't cry that day, but I've done my share of crying at shoots.

The worst time was at our 2009 calendar shoot, actually. The idea was that I was going to be covered in labels. When that didn't work out, I was going to wear a nude swimsuit and have my body painted with 'R's (for Rochelle). I sat there being painted for hours, long into the night. Mine was the last solo of the day and I had to stay the latest. We had started the shoot at 5 a.m., so everyone was exhausted.

Finally, I had my picture taken, in a swimsuit, with 'R's all over me, and my hair pinned to the side. Then I saw a digital still and freaked out: I looked like I was in a shoot for *Zoo* magazine. I really didn't want that. That's when I cried, because I didn't know what to do. I didn't know how we could

change the set-up at the last minute. It was really unlike me, but I think everybody has their moments.

First, I had to have my make-up redone because there was mascara all down my face. Then I said firmly, 'Let's just do a close-up shot.' I had to draw the line and I'm so glad that I did. In the final photo, you can see that I've still got some of the 'R's on me. We are firm believers in speaking out if we don't like what we are doing. There is no point in being fake, putting on a front and saying we like something when we don't. We never start something until everybody is comfortable. We might sometimes

> MOLLIE DIDN'T LIKE HER MAKE-UP, AND VANESSA WASN'T HAPPY WITH THE WAY SHE LOOKED, EITHER. WHEN IT'S YOUR FIRST VIDEO, YOU JUST WANT IT TO BE PERFECT.
> ROCHELLE

WHEN THE PRESSURE IS ON, THOUGH, IT'S EASY TO GET UPSET.

ROCHELLE

annoy a few people, but in the long run everyone gets a better result.

Nicola from Girls Aloud gave us some good advice once, which was basically to trust your instinct. 'If you're not comfortable with something, then don't do it. Everyone wants you to be the best, and you want you to be the best, but if you are not happy doing something, you are not going to be the best.' I always think about that, even when it comes down to what I'm wearing in a shoot. It doesn't matter if someone is saying, 'This is what you should wear. This is what works for you.' If you don't agree, then you should go with your gut instinct and say so. There's no point trying to please other people all the time. You have to stay true to yourself. You know when something is not right, whether it's an outfit, a relationship or a funny-tasting prawn!

FILMING THE FIRST VIDEO WAS AMAZING.

FRANKIE

Vanessa — The first video was so much fun. I loved it. I'd never done a video shoot in my life, so it felt insane! It was slightly scary at first, because we had to perform in front of loads of cameramen and crew. Everyone was looking at us and I was a bit intimidated.

You had to strut your stuff with everyone watching, and the first time I did it was awful. After a few takes, though, I got into it and it was fine after that. These days, we are in front of the camera so much of the time that it's second nature to me. We're good friends with our team and everybody who works with us, so there's no reason to get embarrassed. I didn't feel half so comfortable back then. It was really a case of 'Uh-oh!'

I find it really cringe-making to watch it back now, because I hate the way I look. I don't know exactly why; I just don't like it. I've never been a fan of watching myself on screen, anyway.

Frankie — Filming the first video was amazing. I hadn't done anything like it for a couple of years and doing it again felt so normal and comfortable. At the same time, though, I was nervous because, having done it before, I had something to prove. I was aware that people might say, 'She isn't as good now she's older. She used to be better.'

I love really high shoes, but unfortunately for me, I chose to wear a stupidly high pair for the video. They were really high at the back, high at the front and a size too small. Once I'd worn them for the first set-up, I had to wear them all day, for continuity, so I was walking, dancing and posing in them for seventeen hours! By the end of the day, I was in tears. I couldn't wait to get them off. The Saturdays' colour theme started with the first video. Each of us wore a different-coloured dress, although it wasn't to make a statement. That's just how the director, Harvey B. Brown, wanted it to be.

I LOVE REALLY HIGH SHOES, BUT UNFORTUNATELY FOR ME, I CHOSE TO WEAR A STUPIDLY HIGH PAIR FOR THE VIDEO. THEY WERE REALLY HIGH AT THE BACK, HIGH AT THE FRONT AND A SIZE TOO SMALL.

FRANKIE

Then people started to pick up on it and really liked the idea, because it was something that people could easily copy. No one knows your name at first, but they could identify each of us by colour. 'I like the blue one!' or 'I like the green one!'

We went with it and in the next video, for our second single, 'Up', we all wore different-coloured tights. It was our little iconic touch. JLS then used the same idea. We always joke and say, 'We did it first!' Their colours have stuck with them because they've stuck with their colours, whereas we changed ours around. I didn't want to be blue all of the time. I wanted to be red sometimes. Perhaps we should have kept it the same.

Mollie — The only experience I had of making a video was watching Britney making one on MTV. I'd seen the director saying, 'Cut!' and the clapperboard person saying, 'Take One,' but that was it. So it was all a little overwhelming for me and I started crying. I felt so lost. I didn't feel that I knew what I was doing. I was just so nervous because I really wanted it to be good. After all, a

music video is as important as the song, or that's what I thought at the time.

Making a video sounds easy, but it's not. You've got so many cameras around you! To make it worse, we had pretty much everybody from the label watching us, wanting to see what this new girl band was about and whether we would make the grade. Trying to be sexy, nice and pretty in the space of a three-minute video was scary but amazing at the same time. I didn't feel at all comfortable in front of the camera. I could see that the others were good at giving the camera the eye, and I didn't know how to do that. 'Give me a sexy look now and again,' said Harvey, the director, but I didn't know how to! I felt so inexperienced.

It was the same with our first photo shoots. I'm smiling in every shot. Looking back, you can see the girls around me looking gorgeous and giving it this and that, but I'm just grinning.

Frankie — It was scary releasing the first single, 'If This Is Love'. We had no idea how people

WE ARE FIRM
BELIEVERS IN
SPEAKING OUT IF
WE DON'T LIKE
WHAT WE ARE
DOING. THERE
IS NO POINT IN
BEING FAKE,
PUTTING ON
A FRONT AND
SAYING WE LIKE
SOMETHING
WHEN WE DON'T.
ROCHELLE

WE FEEL WE ARE GETTING THERE NOW, ALTHOUGH
WE STILL GET NERVOUS. IT'S NOT EASY WHEN YOU
HAVEN'T COME THE *X FACTOR* ROUTE, WITH MILLIONS OF
PEOPLE WATCHING YOU EVERY WEEK. IT MAKES IT HARDER
TO RAISE YOUR PROFILE WHEN PEOPLE DON'T KNOW THE
BACKGROUND TO YOUR STORY.

ROCHELLE

were going to react to us, because we'd been in a bubble in the studio. It's a strange situation: you're really excited; you know that everybody in the group is talented; you love your single so much and you've been working on it for so long. Then you suddenly get thrown into the public arena and everyone is checking you out. Do they like you? Do they like your hair? Do they like the song? It was intimidating because people are so quick to laugh and say that you haven't done well.

Rochelle — I was really nervous when our first single came out. I didn't believe we would make the top forty. We are our own biggest critics and our own worst enemies when it comes to being positive. We wind each other up. Once one person says, 'I don't think we'll do well,' it's not long before we all think we're crap. I definitely didn't think we'd get into the top ten, so I was ecstatic when 'If This Is Love' charted at number eight. 'Who bought it?' we kept asking. We were so happy. The only people who knew us were people who had seen us on tour. We must have been doing something right!

By the time we released the second and third singles, things had changed. The phone started ringing with bookings for us to appear on TV shows. That's when we started to feel a bit more comfortable.

We feel we are getting there now, although we still get nervous. It's not easy when you haven't come the *X Factor* route, with millions of people watching you every week. It makes it harder to raise your profile when people don't know the background to your story. I'm just so proud that people know who we are and we are in demand now. It still shocks us that we have come so far. We're all very grounded.

Mollie — The first time we saw the music video for 'If this is Love', I cried. We were at the director's office and I think he was a bit surprised to see me in tears, but it was my first music video, I just loved it!

I was in the kitchen with my mum the first time I saw it on TV. A Madonna video had just played and then it was us. I couldn't believe we were being played after Madonna. My mum and I were screaming. I still get quite excited when any of our videos is on TV.

Una — I don't like the way I look in our first video. I had a fringe that I hated because it wasn't long enough and my hair was straightened. Not a good look. Luckily, for 'Up', I found a hairstyle that suited me.'

> THE FIRST TIME WE SAW THE MUSIC VIDEO FOR 'IF THIS IS LOVE', I CRIED.
> MOLLIE

Frankie — Coming from a band that had done so well, I'd been scared of committing to something else, in case it didn't work out. Luckily, there was a real buzz around us when 'If This Is Love' came out and it was a big success. We must have come along at the right time!

THE SATURDAYS BREAKTHROUGH!

WE HAD A TOP-TEN SINGLE IN THE BAG, BUT WE NEEDED TO CARRY ON DOING WELL IF WE WERE GOING TO STAY AT THE TOP. IN THE NEXT FEW MONTHS, WE WORKED HARDER THAN ANY OF US HAVE EVER WORKED BEFORE, PROMOTING THREE MORE SINGLES (YES, THREE!) AND OUR ALBUM, CHASING LIGHTS. WE WERE DETERMINED TO BUILD ON OUR SUCCESS . . .

Una — We made our mark with our second single, 'Up', a lovely, catchy song that was in the charts for months. The video helped us to develop an image that people really loved. The director, Harvey, came up with the concept of the colours and coloured tights. His creative vision had a huge influence on our subsequent videos and our album covers – in fact, it impacted on the overall image of the band, giving us a distinct and instantly recognisable look.

Mollie — I was a little less nervous making the video for 'Up', but still very scared. It was another really long day. We had to wear heels and my feet were killing me by the time we'd finished. It's a fab Saturdays video: fun, bright and upbeat. We were thrilled when 'Up' got to number five. Another top-ten single and a really great song!

Vanessa — Because we were working so much, I didn't really notice how we appeared from an outsider's point of view. I think it was the same for us all. We sometimes saw ourselves on the telly, but it didn't occur to us that anyone else ever did. That started to change when people began to say,
— 'I've seen you on this and I've seen you on that.'
— 'Really?' I'd say. I never acknowledged it, to be honest. Even now, I find it hard to acknowledge that sort of thing. It's weird. I think we are still stuck in our own little bubble. The first time people recognised us on the street, we were taken by surprise.
— 'Why are those people looking at us? Has one of us got something on our face? What's going on?' As they came closer, Una said, 'Are you all right?' Then it clicked!

I still haven't got used to it. When I'm in my local supermarket, I forget people may recognise me until somebody says,
— 'Are you the girl from the Saturdays?'
— 'Yes, sorry, I am. I forgot about that.' It's weird. I don't think it's something I'll ever get used to, if I'm honest.

WHEN WE WALKED AROUND THE EXHIBITION, PEOPLE WERE POINTING AND SAYING, 'IT'S THE SATURDAYS! THE SATURDAYS!' 'PEOPLE ARE GETTING TO KNOW US!' WE SAID EXCITEDLY.

UNA

Una — We began to be recognised in public around the time we appeared at the Clothes Show Live in Birmingham, in December 2008. We did ten shows a day for a week, performing 'Up' while we danced up and down the catwalk.

When we walked around the exhibition, people were pointing and saying,
— 'It's the Saturdays! The Saturdays!'
— 'People are getting to know us!' we said excitedly.

Frankie — The moment we finished our week at the Clothes Show Live, we drove straight back to London for the Capital FM Jingle-Bell Ball at the O2. That was a really big deal. It was so cool to be asked to do it. There were massive acts appearing and we were playing on the same stage as all these other stars, including Rihanna, Enrique, the Pussycat Dolls and Will Young. It was just unreal.

It was our biggest performance so far, even though we were on the smallest stage, which was about the size of a table for four in a restaurant. We performed 'Up' and we wore huge cloaks covered in sequins. Unfortunately, the sound went wrong before we went on. I couldn't hear anything in my earphones, known as in-ears. Everybody was panicking. We couldn't hold the show up, because it's all timed exactly for the radio. Oh God, it was such a big deal for us. It was our chance to prove ourselves and show that we belonged there. Everyone backstage was screaming,
— 'They can't hear anything in their in-ears!'
Then there was an announcement to say that we were coming on stage, but we weren't ready! What a nightmare. The crowd went mad, but we didn't appear, and by the time we made it on stage, all that excitement had died down.

There we were, in this massive arena, and I had no in-ears, so all I could hear was a series of echoes and white noise. It was horrible. I kept thinking, 'Does anyone realise that I can't hear? Am I singing off-key?' Some of the others had in-ears that were working, but still the sound wasn't good. We were so upset.

I cried afterwards and I wasn't the only one. 'What was that all about?' we shouted. Somebody had really messed up the sound. OK, these things happen, but why did it have to be us? As it turned out, the performance was fine and nobody said anything bad about it, but you always want to feel it's been perfect. We were so disappointed, because it was our big night.

Since then, we have appeared at Capital's Summertime Ball and again at the Jingle-Bell Ball. The more experience we have and the bigger we are, the nicer it is to go back. It just gets better and better.

Vanessa — We did some extra last-minute summer dates with Girls Aloud, which was exciting. We didn't want the tour to end, so it was fantastic that it was extended. Unfortunately, we had a run of bad luck with our gigs in 2008, something always seemed to go wrong around that time. Our in-ears didn't work, or someone's dress strap snapped, or a heel went on someone else's shoe. We did a dance with ribbons for one song and the ribbons would get tangled up and we wouldn't be able to move, because we were stuck. That happened several times; it was awful!

Then our in-ears didn't work at the Jingle-Bell Ball, and what we could hear was all muddled up. We weren't very happy after that performance. We were a bit disheartened by it; we worried that people might have thought that we didn't care about putting in a good performance, when nothing could have been further from the truth.

Mollie — Life just got faster and faster. In January 2009, we released our third single, 'Issues', which got to number four in the charts. Again we were over the moon. We'd had three top-ten singles. Even better, our album, *Chasing Lights*, had gone platinum! As a child, I had always dreamed of getting a plaque commemorating huge record sales. Now my dream had come true!

> WHEN WE WERE TOLD THAT WE'D BEEN PICKED TO DO THE COMIC RELIEF SINGLE, WE STARTED SCREAMING AND GOING CRAZY. 'WOW, WE'VE MADE IT!' IT WAS A HUGE THING FOR US, JUST AMAZING.
> FRANKIE

Rochelle — It was so amazing that we had a platinum album! We were so thrilled!

Mollie — There wasn't time to take it in, though. In the two months after 'Issues' came out, we worked unbelievably hard. Everybody in the industry was commenting on it. I'm not exaggerating – we went for months without a day off and we were starting to feel a bit down.

Frankie — When we were told that we'd been picked to do the Comic Relief single, we started

screaming and going crazy. 'Wow, we've made it!' It was a huge thing for us, just amazing. We chose to record and perform a cover of the Depeche Mode song 'Just Can't Get Enough', which I had always loved. When I look back, I just don't know how we managed to work so hard. We were doing everything.

We did a radio tour and a schools tour, meeting all the kids, as well as visiting a lot of the charities and centres where the Comic Relief money goes. Immediately the tour finished, we did the TV promotion and all the press for that; then the single came out and we had to promote it. We worked solidly for a really long time.

By the end of it, we had got to the point where we were saying,
— 'I'm so tired. I don't think I can do any more.'
I was so exhausted the day we sang live on Comic Relief that I really wasn't in a good space. I didn't even know if I could go on, if I could physically do it. I was at breaking point.

The really tiring part of this job is working every day without a break. We can easily go for a couple of weeks without having a day off, which may not sound too bad if you're working nine to five, because at least you have the evenings off, but for us, it's often all day and all evening too.

Also, you generally know when your holiday is coming up when you work nine to five, so at least

WE DID SOME EXTRA LAST-MINUTE SUMMER DATES WITH GIRLS ALOUD, WHICH WAS EXCITING. WE DIDN'T WANT THE TOUR TO END, SO IT WAS FANTASTIC THAT IT WAS EXTENDED.

VANESSA

you can think, I can't wait till August, when I've got three weeks off. But we don't know when our next day off is going to be, or if we'll even have one. One year, we didn't know how long we were going to have off for Christmas. It's all good, because we moan when we're not busy, but it would be nice if we could find a happy medium.

WE'RE ALL VERY AMBITIOUS.
FRANKIE

We've only got ourselves to blame, really, because we're very aware that every invitation is an opportunity and so we find it hard to turn down offers. Sometimes, if we are offered work when we have been very busy we may think about turning it down.
— 'OK, we won't do it,' we say decisively, thinking about getting that extra bit of sleep, but then we start to think . . . and within no time we're all saying,
— 'Let's do it anyway!' We don't want to miss out; we don't want to look back and say,
— 'We could have done better if we'd made more of an effort.' We're all very ambitious.

Mollie — From when we recorded 'If This Is Love' until the end of our work for Comic Relief and the

IT WAS A VERY EMOTIONAL EXPERIENCE MEETING SO MANY PEOPLE WHO WERE REALLY STRUGGLING IN LIFE, AND MADE US REALISE HOW LUCKY WE ARE.
MOLLIE

promotion for 'Just Can't Get Enough', we probably had just one day off. We worked so hard that we were rundown. We needed a break, but we couldn't have one and we knew it!

Una — We nearly collapsed with exhaustion. Comic Relief was such a good cause and we felt happy to be dedicating so much of our time to charity, but it was an intense schedule. I remember calling my mother on the way back from some shoot at half two in the morning. Obviously, I woke her up.
— 'Mammy, what do I do?' I said. 'Do I go for a shower now, or do I have it at six in the morning, when I get up?' I was so tired that I couldn't make even the tiniest decisions.
— 'Just go to bed now!' she said.

Mollie — We spent two full weeks travelling around the country, visiting many Comic Relief projects, which was a real eye opener, but exhausting too. It was a very emotional experience meeting so many people who were really struggling in life, and made us realise how lucky we are. We had to be on top form, though, because they were so excited about us being there. We wanted to do everything we could to help. Afterwards we were completely shattered. We had given our all.

There was a project in Wandsworth, South-West London, that struck us particularly, because it seemed like a very happy place. It had been set up for people with learning difficulties or troubled backgrounds; it was somewhere they could get away from the worries of everyday life and make music. It really made an impression because the people we met there had the same passions as us. They were all so nice and there was a very

'JUST CAN'T GET ENOUGH' WENT TO NUMBER TWO. WE WERE GUTTED THAT IT DIDN'T MAKE IT TO NUMBER ONE, BUT NEVER MIND! IT WAS OUR BIGGEST SINGLE SO FAR.
VANESSA

light-hearted atmosphere. They were mainly playing drums or guitar, but there was also a guy who wanted to be a rapper and who rapped the most hilarious lyrics. We all just burst out laughing. He loved it and we loved it.

Rochelle — The first place we went to see in Glasgow was a scheme to help young children who had always been in foster homes and weren't doing well at school. It was all about bringing them together with young adults who had been through the same experience and who could mentor them.

It really seemed to be producing results, too. There was a seventeen-year-old helping someone of twelve, and a twenty-one-year-old helping someone of fifteen; it seemed so much more effective than leaving it to teachers, who perhaps might not understand the factors involved because they haven't been in the same situation.

One girl in particular stands out in my memory. She was my age and she had moved sixty times in her life. Sixty times! She was pregnant and already had a child, but she had turned her life around and was just about to buy a house from the council when I met her. She was inspirational.

Mollie — I was excited for weeks about opening Comic Relief. It was a massive event. It meant a lot to me that the Spice Girls had done it and we were following in their footsteps! I had a photo from their performance on my phone; I really worked myself up.

Then, on the morning of the show, I woke up with unbelievable period pains. I couldn't move.

I couldn't even get out of bed. I had no idea what I was going to do!
— 'Don't panic,' said Ruth, from our record company. Everybody was trying to keep us calm because this was the biggest performance of our lives.
— 'I'm going to be there even if I have to sit on the stage without moving,' I said, 'but at the moment I can't move at all.' Thank God for painkillers and a hot-water bottle! Eventually, I began to feel better and managed to make my way in with two hours to spare before we went on.

Everyone's nerves began to build up in the dressing room. We were very conscious that we were going to be singing live in front of millions of people. Still, nothing could ever be as bad as that first show at G-A-Y, as we kept reminding each other! In the end, it went really well. We sang live and it was amazing.

Vanessa — 'Just Can't Get Enough' went to number two. We were gutted that it didn't make it to number one, but never mind! It was our biggest single so far.

> ## I WAS EXCITED FOR WEEKS ABOUT OPENING COMIC RELIEF. IT WAS A MASSIVE EVENT. IT MEANT A LOT TO ME THAT THE SPICE GIRLS HAD DONE IT AND WE WERE FOLLOWING IN THEIR FOOTSTEPS!
> MOLLIE

ROCHELLE

ROCHELLE WISEMAN

I'm too good at shopping.

I'D NEVER GO OUT TO DINNER WITHOUT WEARING HEELS. I'M SO INTO FASHION. I LOVE THE LATE ALEXANDER MCQUEEN, CHANEL AND BALENCIAGA, AND CHRISTIAN LOUBOUTIN FOR SHOES. MY FAVOURITE DRESS IS MY HERVÉ LÉGER BODY-CON.

```
AGE    — 21
BIRTH  — 21 MARCH 1989
SIGN   — ARIES
FROM   — ESSEX
```

About me — I am the shopaholic of the band. I always find a spare minute of the day to buy something. Whether it's in between dance rehearsals or recording at the studio, you'll inevitably catch me at a till point! I'm a real girly girl with a weakness for clothes, shoes and handbags. I tend to be the one who is always early. I have an obsession with being on time! I'm also organised and a tidy freak. I can't stand mess or bad smells!

Favourite items in my wardrobe — My Balenciaga handbag is one of my favourites. I love all of my shoes, so it's hard to pick a favourite pair, but as long as they are high, black and have a platform, I'm happy! I love a high-heel shoe. We have to wear them for work, because you can't really go on stage in a dress and trainers. It's not a look we go for!

I'd never go out to dinner without wearing heels. I'm so into fashion. I love the late Alexander McQueen, Chanel and Balenciaga, and Christian Louboutin for shoes. My favourite dress is my Hervé Léger body-con – it was so expensive, but I love it! Luckily, we can borrow clothes. I always want to take them home, but as soon as I've been pictured in a dress, that's it – I can't really wear it out again, because the press will comment, 'Oh, she wore it again!' It's so annoying! I don't care if I wear something again, but they do. So it's good that people lend us stuff, and Vanessa and I have started to swap with each other.

How do you boost your confidence when you're feeling low? — Find something you are good at, like a hobby. It makes you feel better about yourself if you're doing something well. For a quick fix, have a nice bath. Pamper yourself. Do your hair. Make an effort. If I'm not feeling particularly confident, I always feel better about myself if I've made an effort. Wear something nice, something that you know suits you.

What would you wear on a first date? — Don't look like you have tried too hard! Never turn up in your ball gown. Keep it cool. Wear jeans and heels

I'M A REAL GIRLY GIRL WITH A WEAKNESS FOR CLOTHES, SHOES AND HANDBAGS. I TEND TO BE THE ONE WHO IS ALWAYS EARLY. I HAVE AN OBSESSION WITH BEING ON TIME! I'M ALSO ORGANISED AND A TIDY FREAK.

I'M *TOO* GOOD AT SHOPPING, THAT'S THE PROBLEM! I DON'T USUALLY TRY ANYTHING ON, UNLIKE MOLLIE, WHO WILL BE IN THAT FITTING ROOM THE WHOLE DAY. I TEND TO KNOW IF SOMETHING WILL FIT ME AND I TAKE IT BACK IF IT DOESN'T. I HATE THAT FITTING-ROOM THING, SO I HAVE A LITTLE FASHION SHOW WHEN I GET HOME.

and maybe a plain vest. Don't pretend to like stuff they like if you don't actually like it. I've done that so many times before. It's awful if they then start to talk about it in depth and you're thinking, I don't know what you're talking about. It's definitely not the way to go! It's good to have things in common with someone and you can always tell from the first date whether you have or not. If you haven't, I'd forget it.

Would you kiss on a first date? — If you want to kiss, then kiss! But I don't really like to kiss on a first date. I prefer to keep the mystery and leave them wanting a kiss.

Are you a good shopper? — I'm *too* good at shopping, that's the problem! I don't usually try anything on, unlike Mollie, who will be in that fitting room the whole day. I tend to know if something will fit me and I take it back if it doesn't. I hate that fitting-room thing, so I have a little fashion show when I get home. My best friend, Laura, will often come over and give me her opinion.

Red-carpet tips? — Wear something nice but comfortable when you go to a film première! I always end up wearing something uncomfortable and then I have to go and sit and watch the film for two hours. Also, it's really obvious if you're wearing something uncomfortable when you're posing for the camera. It's no good if you're worrying about pulling this bit down and making sure this bit is tucked in.

When I face the cameras on the red carpet, I give a good mixture of a smile and a pout. They say, 'Show us your dress. Look over your shoulder,' particularly if your dress is backless, but I always feel a bit weird doing an over-the-shoulder pose. It feels as if I have neck ache!

Ever get star-struck? — No, never, even when I meet a big star. It doesn't bother me. Mollie, on the other hand, loves it. We've been at a gig and she's gone up to people's dressing rooms and taken pictures of their names on the door!

I ALWAYS END UP WEARING SOMETHING UNCOMFORTABLE AND THEN I HAVE TO GO AND SIT AND WATCH THE FILM FOR TWO HOURS.

Most embarrassing
moment
—
Falling off
the stage when
I was younger,
in front
of a boy
I really fancied!

How awful!

Favourite
Saturdays Single?
—
'Issues'
I just love
that song!

On my iPod
—
Alicia Keys,
Jazmine Sullivan
and Rihanna.
I also like a lot
of stuff my mum
was listening to
when I was younger,
like Elton John,
Rod Stewart and
Lionel Richie.

Would you kiss
on a first date?
—
If you want
to kiss, then kiss!
But I don't really
like to kiss on
a first date.

Interesting fact
—

In 2007, I entered the Miss England competition, thinking that at the very least it might add to my modelling portfolio. I was amazed to reach the final, but I backed out when the audition for the Saturdays came up. Being in a band is where I belong.

Favourite Saturdays video?
—

I loved making the 'Just Can't Get Enough' video, because we got to play around and do a little bit of acting.

Five words that describe me best
—

Girly
Crazy
Sensitive
Mummy's girl
Caring

Ever have a clothes crisis?
—

I often think I haven't got anything to wear. (I know!) That is what is good about having a best friend who also loves her clothes. She has half my wardrobe at her house and vice versa.

FIND SOMETHING YOU ARE GOOD AT, LIKE A HOBBY. IT MAKES YOU FEEL BETTER ABOUT YOURSELF IF YOU'RE DOING SOMETHING WELL. FOR A QUICK FIX, HAVE A NICE BATH. PAMPER YOURSELF. DO YOUR HAIR. MAKE AN EFFORT.

EVERYBODY SAID MY TWENTY-FIRST BIRTHDAY WAS LIKE A WEDDING. I WORE A BEAUTIFUL DRESS WITH A LONG TRAIN. UNFORTUNATELY, ONE OF THE PAPARAZZI PHOTOGRAPHERS STOOD ON THE TRAIN AND RIPPED IT JUST AS I WAS GOING INTO THE HOTEL FOR THE PARTY! I HAD NO IDEA HE WAS ON IT AT ALL, SO I CARRIED ON WALKING AND IT RIPPED RIGHT UP THE BUM! SO I WAS TWO HOURS LATE FOR MY PARTY BECAUSE I HAD TO GO BACK AND BE SEWN INTO THE DRESS!

Fashion advice? — Whatever the fashion is, always stick to your body shape. I know what I can and can't wear. I've got boobs and I've got a bum, so I don't wear baggy stuff because it just tents out and makes me look bigger than I am. Something waisted and quite tailored looks a lot better on me. That's why I love body-con dresses, because you can see my figure. If I wear something looser, it can put two stone on me, which is not necessary!

Wardrobe malfunction? — Everybody said my twenty-first birthday was like a wedding. I wore a beautiful dress with a long train. Unfortunately, one of the paparazzi photographers stood on the train and ripped it just as I was going into the hotel for the party! I had no idea he was on it at all, so I carried on walking and it ripped right up the bum! So I was two hours late for my party because I had to go back and be sewn into the dress!

Apart from that, though, it was a fantastic night. We had a great old time, me and the girls. Everyone was there, from my family and the people I grew up with to my old dance teachers. I hired a private room so that we could relax without worrying about being watched. It was nice not to be asked for pictures all night, for once. Although it's great to be asked, after a while you want to be with your friends and enjoy yourself.

That's why I think the girls had a good night, because we knew everyone in there, through work and my family, and they certainly don't care, so everyone was letting loose and going for it.

WHATEVER THE FASHION IS, ALWAYS STICK TO YOUR BODY SHAPE. I KNOW WHAT I CAN AND CAN'T WEAR. I'VE GOT BOOBS AND I'VE GOT A BUM, SO I DON'T WEAR BAGGY STUFF BECAUSE IT JUST TENTS OUT AND MAKES ME LOOK BIGGER THAN I AM.

THE SATURDAYS
THE WORK TOUR

IN THE SUMMER OF 2009, WE GOT THE CHANCE TO DO WHAT WE LOVE BEST – AGAIN AND AGAIN! PERFORMING IS AND ALWAYS WILL BE OUR FAVOURITE THING IN THE WORLD. THE WORK TOUR TOOK US ALL AROUND THE COUNTRY AND GAVE US THE CHANCE TO MEET AND CONNECT WITH OUR FANS. IT WAS BRILLIANT!

Rochelle — We had a debate about what to name the tour and each of us came up with different suggestions. *Chasing Lights* was the name of our first album, but it sounded a bit clichéd for a tour, so we decided against it. Even before we decided to release 'Work' as our fifth single, we thought calling it 'the Work Tour' might be good. We visualised scaffolding and industrial sounds; we thought it would be cool to toughen up the Saturdays' profile. And so that's what we went for in the end.

We didn't really do a lot of promotion for the 'Work' single. That's partly because we weren't originally going to release another single from the album. But then, since we had recorded it, we said, 'Shall we just see how it does?' When it came to the actual release date, everyone had already bought it as a download from the album, so it only reached number twenty-two!

Mollie — Usually, you have three weeks to rehearse for a tour, but we were given ten days!

Even our choreographer, Paul Domaine, felt the pressure. 'Girls, we are really pushed for time here, so you are going to put on your thinking caps and get these routines into your heads.'

Those rehearsals were so exciting. Knowing we were going on our own tour really focused our minds. It was mayhem, though. There was so much to take in. We met the live band and rehearsed with them; we tried to work out the order of the songs and what we would say on stage. Most days the girls brought their dogs into work with them, so we'd be in the middle of intense singing and dancing lessons with the dogs running around everywhere. To make matters worse we lost our stylist the week before our first night. We had five days to go and nothing to wear! Fortunately, we had just done a campaign with Rare Fashion and they came up trumps, along with Lipsy and a Spanish company called Collado Garcia. They were all so good to us and sent us some lovely dresses.

WE ARE FIVE GIRLS WHO ALL LIKE FASHION, SO WE CAN VERY WELL COME IN ONE DAY AND ALL WANT TO WEAR THE SAME OUTFIT.

ROCHELLE

Even so, we still had a problem with our opening outfits, so we sat down with some designers and discussed what would look good on stage. After deciding on a silver theme, they asked us what shape and design we were looking for. Well, although we love fashion, we are not designers, so we had some problems! I wanted my dress to be heart-shaped and strapless, which worked fine until the dress rehearsal, when it became clear it needed straps!

∞

Things got worse. Some of the outfits just didn't fit the others, so we had to mix and match, improvise and rely on last-minute inspiration. The day before our first night, we dropped the dresses and did our rehearsal in American Apparel leotards with skirts and shorts, which we'd bought at the eleventh hour. When Peter, head of Fascination saw us, he said,
— 'You cannot wear that!'
— 'We've got nothing to wear! What are we going to do?'

∞

Finally, all the dresses that had ever been made for us were sent up to Glasgow, where the first show was. Thankfully, the colour schemes were all quite similar and we managed to put together a silvery theme for the opening part of the show. Vanessa, Frankie and I wore silver dresses; Rochelle wore a plain cream tube dress and eventually Una went out and bought her outfit from Jane Norman. That's typical of Una:
— 'My dress doesn't fit and I'll sort it out myself!'

∞

Amazingly, we pulled it off and everybody thought that the opening outfits were planned. Everything else fitted us fine, so we didn't have any more problems. It's funny to look back on, but it certainly wasn't funny at the time. Lots of tears and tantrums! It was a complete nightmare. Actually, we've got an incredible stylist now and I'm sure our outfits will be amazing when we tour again.

Rochelle — There is always a problem with the costumes when you've got five people to keep happy! It's just life, isn't it? We are a stylist's nightmare, a make-up artist's nightmare and a hairdresser's nightmare. We are five girls who all like fashion, so we can very well come in one day and all want to wear the same outfit. Obviously, we can't wear the same thing, so the stylist has to say,
— 'I think this will work best on you.'

♫

In true Saturdays' style, we didn't have an opening costume until the day before our first show. It was hell for me, being the tidy, organised and on-time freak that I am. I couldn't sleep the night before. Even when we flew to Glasgow on the day of the show, I wasn't a hundred per cent sure what I was wearing. It was hands-on that day. Half an hour before we went on, Jayne was still sticking diamanté crystals on my dress. It was just awful.
I was shaking in the corner!

Una — We started working for the tour with our choreographer, Paul Domaine. He really helped me improve my dancing and he always says to me now, 'Don't ever say you can't dance.' Our team on tour was the best: Nicky Tours for hair, Celena for make-up and Luan, our stylist, helped with the quick changes between songs. That time on tour was probably the best part of my life.

It was so fantastic to be doing what I love. Looking out on the first night at Glasgow and seeing all those little girls waving their sparklers and singing along to our songs was incredible! It reminded me of when I was a Eurovision backing singer in 2006. 'Wow!' I thought. 'I can't believe this is happening!' I still pinch myself sometimes when I'm doing big events. Performing with a live band – Dave, Jimmy, Jonas and Damon – was so amazing.

This was the first time we really got to know our fans. Many came to several dates and by the end of the tour we knew loads of their names. We are blessed to have such loyal fans.

It was surreal. People had actually bought tickets to come and see us, and they knew all the words to our songs! In Cardiff, we performed in the arena where we had opened for Girls Aloud the year before, but this time we filled the arena for ourselves. That was really something. I just want to be back on tour. That's how good it was. Being in the band has opened so many doors

to me as a performer. If I was ever to end up a solo artist, I wouldn't be hiding behind a guitar any more. I would actually be able to give a proper performance! I didn't know how to work the stage and the audience, before the band. It's not something someone can teach you. It's just experience and confidence; the more you do it, the more at ease you feel. I got to play guitar in the acoustic section along with Mollie. We had sister guitars. Hers was blonde and mine was brunette.

Rochelle — I enjoyed our own tour better than any shared gig we have ever done. It's great performing at a shared gig, but everybody else's fans are there along with yours, whereas when it's your own tour, it's your crowd and they're there for you. They are screaming and going for it because they have paid to watch you. Before the tour started, I said to Jayne,
— 'I wonder if anybody will turn up.'
— 'Rochelle, the tour has sold out!' she laughed.
— 'That's what they say, but will anyone actually

> # I STILL PINCH MYSELF SOMETIMES WHEN I'M DOING BIG EVENTS.
> UNA

come?' It was weird. It only sank in when I went out there on the first night and saw a sea of fans shouting for us. 'OK! They did turn up!'
My mum cried and so did her best friend, Sharon. Mum comes to the first night of everything we do. She was at the first G-A-Y, the first time we supported Girls Aloud and the first night of our tour. She will often be at the second and the third night too, basically, she's there all the time; but she always makes sure she comes to the first! In Glasgow, on our opening night, she came along to see me and called me in tears, just before we

I REALLY
ENJOYED
OUR TOUR.
IT WAS SO
FANTASTIC
TO BE DOING
WHAT I LOVE.
ROCHELLE

went on. I was oblivious, trying to do everything I could to get ready. 'What's wrong?' I asked. It didn't occur to me that that she might be crying because she was overwhelmed.

— 'Mum, is everything all right? I'm sending Mark to come out and get you.' Mark is our tour manager.

— 'No, no, I'm crying because I just saw a little girl buy a Saturdays' T-shirt.'

— 'Yes,' I said, waiting for her to get to the point.

— 'Well, I can't believe that little girls are buying T-shirts with you girls on.'

— 'Mum, I'll have to call you back. I'm going on in five minutes. We can reminisce afterwards.'

— 'Oh, I'm sorry, I didn't realise!'

> # I DO THIS JOB BECAUSE I LOVE PERFORMING.
> FRANKIE

She's so funny. If I wave at the crowd anywhere in her direction, she'll wave back. Afterwards, she'll say,

— 'I saw you waving!' I say,

— 'No, Mum, I wasn't waving at you. You don't need to be waved at. I was waving at that little girl near you.'

Frankie — I do this job because I love performing. Being on stage and doing my thing is just amazing. That's why I went to stage school. *The X Factor* wasn't around in those days, so my original aim was to be in theatre. When I got into a pop group, I kept at it because of the performing aspect. Even today, we just do the interviews and the promotion to get us to a place where we are the biggest and the best we can be.

I'm in it to perform. It's funny, because there are times when I'm so tired and fed up that I can't be bothered to put my make-up on, or a blooming tight dress, or something revealing. I'm thinking, I can't do it. I can't go on there. I'm too tired. Then the instant I get out there, I feel amazing and I forget. That's what I love.

There's a big difference between the Saturdays performing and the Saturdays relaxing. When we're backstage, we can get a bit stupid and mess around. We often don't wear our make-up and sometimes we don't look that great, so it's nice to see how we transform. It's just like girls doing themselves up on a Saturday night. We like to look hot and feel good. It's fun getting dressed up, although you get used to it after a while. It can get a bit boring sitting in the make-up chair for an hour and a half. I'm only twenty-one. I think, do I really need that much make-up?

Vanessa — The first night of the Work Tour was amazing. I've never felt so good. It was in Glasgow and we love Glasgow. The fans there are fantastic, so to have our first night there was great. It was a big deal to go from supporting Girls Aloud to headlining our own tour. We couldn't believe it. Before the tour started, we'd all said, 'What if we get up there and there are only five people in the audience?' We didn't think anyone really knew about us, so it was insane when we saw how packed the venues were and when we had to add dates to the tour. We were all so happy.

I had a piece of bad luck on the second night, though. As I was climbing some stairs to join the girls on the top of some scaffolding, I tripped over a loose wire, buckled in my heels and bent my ankle back on itself. It was so painful! I can't describe how bad it was. I started screaming, 'Oh my God!' I couldn't walk; I couldn't move, because I was in so much agony. If only that wire had been taped down! When the song started, I panicked. I was still backstage! Jayne rushed up to help me.

— 'What do I do?' I asked her through my tears.

— 'Just keep singing,' she said, pointing at the microphone in my hand.

I did my best, but the pain was so bad that it was hard to carry on. After what seemed like ages, but was probably only a minute, Jayne said,

— 'OK, you can stop singing now.' Then Rochelle

THERE'S A BIG DIFFERENCE BETWEEN THE SATURDAYS PERFORMING AND THE SATURDAYS RELAXING. WHEN WE'RE BACKSTAGE, WE CAN GET A BIT STUPID AND MESS AROUND.

FRANKIE

took over my parts, and later on Una also helped out. I think there were a few hiccups, but it was basically fine.

There were paramedics backstage who dealt with my ankle. Then they put me in a wheelchair and told me not to move. Well, I was in so much pain that I couldn't move; I wasn't going anywhere!

After a while, though, I couldn't bear being backstage any longer. The girls were out front, doing their stuff, and I felt I was missing out. I also felt bad that I hadn't shown up when I tripped on the stairs. I needed to do something, so towards the end of the show I was wheeled on to the stage, while the girls were singing a cover of 'Shut Up and Drive' by Rihanna.

> THERE WERE PARAMEDICS BACKSTAGE WHO DEALT WITH MY ANKLE. THEN THEY PUT ME IN A WHEELCHAIR AND TOLD ME NOT TO MOVE. WELL, I WAS IN SO MUCH PAIN THAT I COULDN'T MOVE; I WASN'T GOING ANYWHERE!
>
> VANESSA

What a great moment! I started singing as I came on and the girls all turned to look at me in amazement. I quickly described what had happened and we finished the show together. The following evening and for most of the shows after that, I had to sit on a stool at the back of the stage.

It was nice, but I got a little bit frustrated. I just wanted to be dancing with the girls, but at least I did do all of the shows one way or another.

Rochelle — Vanessa fell as she was walking up the stairs behind me, so I saw it, but the other girls didn't because they were already on stage. I made a quick decision to stand in her place until she made it up the stairs, but then she didn't come up. I kept looking to see where she was, until Mark, our tour manager, whispered, 'No, she's not coming.'

> WHAT A GREAT MOMENT! I STARTED SINGING AS I CAME ON AND THE GIRLS ALL TURNED TO LOOK AT ME IN AMAZEMENT.
>
> VANESSA

When I started singing Vanessa's bit, the other girls looked round at me, astonished.
— 'Vanessa's ill,' I murmured in between songs. 'Don't worry, I'm not being greedy!' It was hard work that night, because I had to do my stuff and her stuff as well. Usually, you only think about what you need to do as part of the team, but suddenly I had to think about two people, so I was everywhere.
— 'You're doing a good job,' our manager told me through my earpiece. 'Carry on doing Vanessa's bits. She will not be back on.'

It was good to know I was doing OK, but I was worried about Vanessa. Then, just before the last song, I explained to the audience what had happened. The fans wanted to see her, so they wheeled her on in a wheelchair at the end of the show.

WE DIDN'T
THINK ANYONE
REALLY KNEW
ABOUT US, SO
IT WAS INSANE
WHEN WE SAW
HOW PACKED
THE VENUES
WERE AND WHEN
WE HAD TO ADD
DATES TO THE
TOUR. WE WERE
ALL SO HAPPY.
VANESSA

— 'Hi, everyone. Sorry I couldn't do the show,' she said. Poor thing, she was in a bad way and it was horrible for her. There were paramedics all around her and she was worried that she wouldn't be able to do any of the subsequent shows.

She couldn't do anything for herself that night. I had to lift her into the shower and put her on the toilet. I've seen it all! I was her carer for the rest of the tour, pushing her around in the wheelchair. At the airport, I'd say, 'Excuse me, lady coming through!' It meant that we went through check-in more quickly. I was like, 'Go on, girl.'

But then she'd call me from her room at night and say,
— 'I'm in bed, but I really want a drink.'
— 'All right, I'm on my way.' I was like her mum.

Vanessa — It was awful not being independent. Every time I wanted to do anything, I needed three people to help me out of the chair. That first night, Rochelle had to sit me on the loo and Jayne helped me to brush my teeth. I had to be pushed around, lifted into cars and on to planes, and helped into bed. I hated it.

I went to see a doctor as soon as I could. He gave me acupuncture, sticking the needles right into my ankle, which killed. He also gave me ultrasound treatment, which felt very strange, as if something was pulling my ankle from the inside. Then he did something weird called cupping, which is a method of drawing blood to the surface of the skin using heated cups. The heat creates a partial vacuum, which means that the cup sucks on to the swelling, helping it to go down. I didn't like it much, especially the time he put eight cups all the way up my leg. That was very painful! I dreaded going to see him, but he was amazing and cut the recovery time in half.

Towards the end of the tour, I started telling myself that I could get up and dance again.

ON OUR NIGHTS OFF FROM OUR TOUR, WE SUPPORTED TAKE THAT FOR FIVE NIGHTS ON THEIR CIRCUS STADIUM TOUR. IT WAS AMAZING.
ROCHELLE

— 'No, you are not doing it,' everyone said. 'You haven't healed properly yet.' I was so frustrated. I really wanted to get back out there.

I was the one wearing the highest heels at the start of the tour, but when I finally went back to dancing, I had to wear the ugliest pair of low-heeled shoes you've ever seen. The other four wore them because it was easier to dance in them, but being short, I wanted shoes that would give me some height. 'I don't care if they hurt; I just want to look good dancing,' I said. So I was rather upset when I had to settle for the ugly low heels.

Rochelle — On our nights off from our tour, we supported Take That for five nights on their Circus stadium tour. It was amazing. I was the biggest Take That fan growing up, so although I don't usually get star-struck, it was a huge deal for me. The first night, their manager told our manager,
— 'The boys want to meet the girls,' so we went to their dressing room and knocked on the door. The tour manager said,
— 'The Saturdays are here to see you.'

I was really nervous as we went in. It felt like we were going to see the Queen. What are they going to be like? I wondered. Why do they want to meet us? As it turned out, they were the nicest, friendliest people I've ever met.
— 'I'm documenting the tour,' Gary Barlow said. 'Would it be OK to get a picture with you?'
We thought, 'Would you mind if *we* get a picture with *you*, more like!'

ON OUR
NIGHTS OFF
FROM OUR
TOUR, WE
SUPPORTED
TAKE THAT
FOR FIVE
NIGHTS ON
THEIR CIRCUS
STADIUM TOUR.
IT WAS
AMAZING.
ROCHELLE

WE WENT TO ASIA TWICE. THE FIRST TIME, WE SPENT
A FEW DAYS IN MALAYSIA. THE SECOND TIME, IT
WAS FOR A WEEK AND A HALF IN KUALA LUMPUR IN
MALAYSIA, MANILA IN THE PHILIPPINES, AND BANGKOK
IN THAILAND. IT WAS AMAZING.
VANESSA

Unfortunately, I fell over on stage while we were performing 'I Just Can't Get Enough'. We do a dance with a chair during the song: we have to spin round on a chair and then sit back down on it. Well, I was so into it and excited that I span round, fell legs akimbo and landed on my bum on the stage, and the chair came down with me. In front of sixty thousand people!

— 'Did anyone see that?' I asked the girls afterwards.

— 'Yeah!' they said in unison.

— 'Why? Was it on the screen?' Of course it was Sod's Law that they chose to film me just as I fell!

— 'Oh, no, Gary's not going to think I am cool any more.'

Vanessa's reaction was the best. She was sitting on a stool because she couldn't dance, so she saw everything. She was nearly peeing herself with laughter.

> VANESSA'S REACTION
> WAS THE BEST. SHE WAS
> NEARLY PEEING HERSELF
> WITH LAUGHTER.
> ROCHELLE

Mollie — After the tour we had seven days off and then we went straight off to Asia for twelve days, which was amazing. We went to Malaysia, Thailand and the Philippines. I was expecting it to be like Japan, where I visited my dad when he was working there for a year, but of course each country is completely different. It was a huge learning experience for us.

It was quite hard, too. We had just come off the tour, which had already involved being away from home for a few weeks, and now we were away again. We all suffered bad jet lag and had trouble adjusting to the time difference. It was also really hot out there, which made things like hair and make-up so much more difficult. Our make-up trickled off our faces in the heat, our hair went flat, and we were constantly sweating. We weren't on top form at all. Still, we knew how important it was to make a good impression and so we worked hard.

The fans were fantastic over there. They had obviously done their research, because we hadn't had much presence in Malaysia, Thailand and the Philippines. In the UK, whether you like us or not, most weeks you'll come across one of us when you open a magazine. There was nothing like that out East, but the fans had taken an interest and it was clear that they knew a lot about us. That meant so much to us and it was great to meet them. I was quite homesick, though. I missed my mum, and while I was away, I fell out with my boyfriend, which made it even tougher. We made it up when I got home, though!

> WE WEREN'T ON TOP
> FORM AT ALL. STILL, WE
> KNEW HOW IMPORTANT
> IT WAS TO MAKE A GOOD
> IMPRESSION.
> MOLLIE

MANILA SEEMED VERY AMERICANISED. THERE WAS AN INSANE AMOUNT OF TRAFFIC AND WE HAD TO GET POLICE ESCORTS EVERYWHERE TO GET THROUGH IT, OTHERWISE YOU'D BE STUCK FOR AN HOUR JUST TRYING TO GET ROUND A CORNER. EVERYTHING ELSE WAS GREAT, THOUGH. I LOVE THE PEOPLE THERE AND THE FOOD.
VANESSA

Vanessa — We went to Asia twice. The first time, we spent a few days in Malaysia. The second time, it was for a week and a half in Kuala Lumpur in Malaysia, Manila in the Philippines, and Bangkok in Thailand. It was amazing, even though most of us were sick and jet-lagged. I wish we'd been able to absorb it more, so I'm looking forward to going back and having more time there, when we're not tired or ill.

My mum is Filipino and I've been to the Philippines loads. I love it – not so much Manila, the capital, but the beach at Boracay is like paradise. I was really excited before we flew there.
— 'I'm going home!' I kept saying. The girls laughed at me.
— 'This is your home, you loser!'
— 'OK, but I stayed in the Philippines for three months when I was younger and I learned to speak the language fluently,' I retorted.

However, when we got there, I found that I had forgotten how to speak Filipino, although I knew lots of words. I could understand what people were saying, but I couldn't speak back.

Manila seemed very Americanised. There was an insane amount of traffic and we had to get police escorts everywhere to get through it, otherwise you'd be stuck for an hour just trying to get round a corner. Everything else was great, though. I love the people there and the food.

Mum used to cook Filipino food when I was growing up. She still does, but mostly on special occasions. Now and again I say,
— 'I really feel like having adobo chicken and rice, please, Mum.'
It comes with the most delicious ginger, garlic and soy sauce. There is lots of vinegar in it, which sounds weird, but it's delicious. Mum used to make noodles all the time, but not so much now.
— 'I really miss your special noodles,' I say. 'Can you make them for me?'
So I loved our trip to the Philippines, because I had the chance to eat all my favourite childhood dishes!

IT WAS ALSO REALLY HOT OUT THERE, WHICH MADE THINGS LIKE HAIR AND MAKE-UP SO MUCH MORE DIFFICULT. OUR MAKE-UP TRICKLED OFF OUR FACES IN THE HEAT, OUR HAIR WENT FLAT, AND WE WERE CONSTANTLY SWEATING.
MOLLIE

THE SATURDAYS
GIRLS IN LOVE

WHAT CAN WE SAY? WE LOVE BEING IN LOVE...

Frankie — I was one of those girls who always had a boyfriend when I was at school. I had a new one every couple of weeks! I liked the cool guys at school; I thought it was important to be with someone cool. Funnily enough, the guys who were cool then are the ones who have turned out to be a bit lame now. Although I am a big flirt, I'm really picky. I've never been one of those girls who goes out on loads of dates. I've got friends who will go out with anyone who asks them: 'Yes, might as well. It's a free drink!' But I don't see it like that.

o—

Some of my friends go around snogging boys in clubs. I would never do that, because for me, kissing someone is a big deal. I am romantic and I like the feeling of being taken out for a nice dinner and having a guy look after you. I don't feel I have to be spoiled or that they should buy me loads of stuff, but the little things count. I like a bit of romance.

o—

I don't go out on loads of dates, because I don't see the point if I'm going to sit there and get bored. If the guy is funny, then OK, but if I'm not sure about him, I'd rather be with my friends than have dinner with somebody who is boring the arse off me. The pressure! The awkwardness! I like being comfortable. I like being able to say what I want to say and be myself.

Guys don't quite know what they are letting themselves in for with me. I do like to be treated well, but I don't like someone who is going to let me walk all over them, either. I will push it if I can. I hate being stifled.

o—

I was fourteen when I started going out with my first proper boyfriend. His family were friends of my family and they lived a road away from us. His name was Mark and he was lovely. I remember thinking that he was so grown-up because he was sixteen. At the time, I thought our relationship was very serious. I suppose it was, for our age. (It's funny, because my cousin is fourteen now and the thought of her having a boyfriend freaks me out, because she seems so young!) I was with him until I was seventeen, so we were together for a long time. We got on really, really well and went on holidays together. Back then, I seriously thought I could marry him – as you do. My family loved him. They're not gushy types, but I think even they thought that I'd found my soul mate.

o—

When it ended with S Club Juniors, I became very reliant on Mark because I didn't have a group of friends. Then, slowly, I began to feel that I needed to go and do my own thing for a while. He went to university but we stayed together for the first year that he was away.

I WAS FOURTEEN WHEN I STARTED GOING OUT WITH MY FIRST PROPER BOYFRIEND. HIS FAMILY WERE FRIENDS OF MY FAMILY AND THEY LIVED A ROAD AWAY FROM US. HIS NAME WAS MARK AND HE WAS LOVELY.

FRANKIE

Then we broke up mutually and stayed friends. He still lives close to my family and I hear his news, but I haven't seen him for a while. Neither of us felt heartbroken when we split up, probably because we thought we would get back together at some point. I sometimes wonder if it's weird for him that I'm in The Saturdays now, and how he feels when he sees that I've been voted one of the World's Sexiest Women by *FHM* (even though it's completely mad!). It must be quite hard for ex-boyfriends, because they can't get away from you. Someone's always going to ask them about you. Still, maybe it can also be quite nice, a bit of street cred!

A year after I broke up with Mark, I went out with a guy called James for six months. We had a lot of fun together and he introduced me to loads of different music. That was an interesting time for me.

In July 2008, I started going out with Dougie from the band McFly. Dougie and I had always fancied each other, even though we'd never met. I knew some of the other boys in his band, but I'd never met him. He used to say in interviews that he fancied me and I always said I fancied him. This went on for years and I felt certain that I'd be with him at some point.

I finally met him at a gig the Saturdays did at G-A-Y – not the first one we did (thank goodness, as we were all mortified after that!), but one we did later on. We were introduced and he shook my hand, which was really awkward.
— 'You all right?' he asked.
— 'Ye-ah,' I replied nervously.
— 'Are you just gonna shake her hand?' said Harry, one of his bandmates.
— 'Um . . .' Dougie and I mumbled.

He got my number from our tour manager and we started texting. I was really, really nervous before our first date, which was at a restaurant in Covent Garden; I was scared that it might be a let-down. I felt I had a lot to live up to and I was worried

that he wasn't going to like my new short haircut, because my hair had always been long and he used to say how much he liked it!

Thankfully, the date wasn't a let-down at all. We instantly clicked and it ended up being better than either of us had expected. We had such a nice time and found so much to talk about that we were in the restaurant for ages. In the end, we were asked to leave because everyone else had gone and they wanted to close. They had been packing up around us and we hadn't even noticed!

Dougie and I had liked each other for so long that it was like, 'Oh, we are finally together!' He was my first boyfriend in the music industry and it was nice to be with somebody who understood what I was doing. We had a real connection because we had both been performing from such a young age.

> DOUGIE AND I HAD LIKED EACH OTHER FOR SO LONG THAT IT WAS LIKE, 'OH, WE ARE FINALLY TOGETHER!'
> FRANKIE

The only difference was that I'd had a break between S Club Juniors and the Saturdays, but McFly had been together the whole time, since Dougie was fifteen. He knew the industry inside out and he taught me a lot.

I always think if someone can make you laugh and make you feel comfortable, then that is love. Dougie just had that something that made me feel happy. There were other things that connected us: he was into skateboarding and I loved that; he had lizards and I love lizards and frogs. Stuff like that – stupid things. Plus, most of the boys I knew of his age didn't have their own place to live, and he had his own dog, too, which was nice. After we'd been

going out for a while, I decided that I wanted to move out of home. Since he didn't want to be on his own any more, I moved in with him. Everything seemed perfect. It felt a bit weird that everybody knew we were together, but because I was happy, I didn't care, even when I got stick from his fans.

o—

Still, I hadn't realised just how interested people are in your personal life. Back when I was in S Club Juniors, journalists weren't allowed to write about me in that way, because of my age.

o—

When Dougie and I broke up for a couple of months, I understood what being in the public eye really meant. I thought, 'Oh crap. People want to know all about us.'

o—

You read all this stuff about other celebrities, but I just didn't think we'd be written about in the same way. Perhaps I was being naïve. I found it strange that people were so interested. They immediately wanted to know why we had broken up. They wanted to uncover something scandalous, so they dug around, trying to find out if one of us had done something wrong.

o—

It was bad enough trying to get used to the fact that I had broken up with the guy I'd been living with, but when the whole country wants to know what's going on, it's really difficult. I felt like saying, 'I don't even know myself! I haven't figured it out in my own head.'

o—

Did we break up because we started living together too soon? Actually, living together was not the problem. We got on fine. We never argued. We broke up on good terms. Was I looking for someone else? Definitely not. I just felt that I wanted some time and the independence of having my own flat. I certainly didn't want another boyfriend. My life was full enough; I was very busy. It was a very hard decision to make, because nothing was particularly wrong. As it turned out, we both missed each other like crazy and decided to get back together.

When you break up with someone, the papers try to pin you with other people. Now that's hurtful, not so much for you, but for the other person involved. I don't care who people think I'm with. But what about your ex? How is he supposed to feel when he opens the paper and sees a story about you with someone else?

> YOU HAVE TO LEARN TO CUT OFF BUT, BECAUSE THIS WAS THE FIRST TIME IT HAD HAPPENED TO ME, I FELT QUITE SHOCKED AND IT REALLY AFFECTED ME.
> FRANKIE

Dougie was pictured at Nobu with one of the girls in my old band. She was there with someone else, but in the pictures they made it look like they were together, so I got up one morning and saw him with someone else. Great. He can do what he wants, but it isn't nice to see and it's even worse if it's not true. Then I was linked with one of the guys in JLS, Aston, even though he's simply my friend. For Dougie, that was horrible. He didn't want to see that. When you break up with someone in a normal situation, you can go on dates and do what you want without either of you knowing what the other one is doing. It was different for us: we knew exactly what the other one was doing all of the time, and everybody was waiting for something to happen. The paps will constantly be trying to catch you with someone and make it look like you're on a date with them, whether you are or not.

o—

When you are trying to get over each other and not be in touch, because it's easier that way, you'd rather not be texting each other to say, 'There's a story coming out today. It's not true.' It makes it harder to move away from each other. As much as I know that a lot of what you read isn't true – and even if something doesn't sound true – it's always going to put doubt in my mind. I'm a

I MOVED IN WITH HIM. EVERYTHING SEEMED PERFECT. IT FELT A BIT WEIRD THAT EVERYBODY KNEW WE WERE TOGETHER, BUT BECAUSE I WAS HAPPY, I DIDN'T CARE, EVEN WHEN I GOT STICK FROM HIS FANS,

FRANKIE

trusting person, but a part of me still thinks, 'Well, maybe . . . ' That's the horrible thing. I guess it's the same for everyone in the public eye, although it's on a totally different scale for someone like Cheryl Cole. I don't know how she deals with it.

∘—

You have to learn to cut off, but because this was the first time it had happened to me, I felt quite shocked and it really affected me. I just didn't realise people were that interested in my life! Luckily, I went on holiday at the right time, but I was still getting phone calls.
— 'This has come out in the press today. Is it true?'
— 'No, it's not!' I shouldn't read the papers, but I can't help wanting to know what people have said about me. I want to know what's been put out there and what people are thinking, even though it doesn't matter what people say, whether it's true or not. I can't help it, though. Anyway, even if you don't read the papers and magazines, someone will always say,
— 'I heard this story on the radio, Frankie. Is it is true?'
— 'No, Uncle Paul, it's not.' You can't get away from it! I find it hard to believe when a celebrity says

they don't know what's written about them because they don't read it. After all, everyone else around them has read it.

∘—

What's weird is that you can say that something is not true until you're blue in the face, but people will believe it anyway. For instance, the papers said that Aston and I were 'good friends' – and that's what we are, good friends! – but everyone knows what they are implying, and that's why the papers have said it like that.

∘—

I was also linked with Calum Best at one point. They said, 'They hooked up.' We tried to get them

> YOU CAN FALL DEEPLY IN LOVE WITH SOMEONE WHO MAKES YOU LAUGH, BECAUSE THEY INSTANTLY PUT YOU IN A GOOD MOOD.
> UNA

to retract that suggestion, because it wasn't true, but they said,
— 'Well, we didn't say you were together.'
— 'You said that we hooked up!' I said.
— 'It's a loose term that doesn't mean anything.'
But everybody knows what 'hooked up' means. They choose their words very carefully. They write things like, 'A pal says . . .' or 'A close friend said . . .', when in fact no close friend of mine said anything!

Una — I was going through my rebellious phase at school when I met my first love. I was sixteen and he was eighteen and it felt like he was so much older than me because he was two years ahead of me at school and really cool. He was a very funny person. That's what I like most, somebody who makes me laugh. You can fall deeply in love with someone who makes you laugh, because they instantly put you in a good mood. Then you feel good about yourself and forget everything else. I thought he was the most gorgeous person in the world because I loved his personality so much.

> # I WAS GOING THROUGH MY REBELLIOUS PHASE AT SCHOOL WHEN I MET MY FIRST LOVE.
> UNA

My boyfriend now, Ben, really makes me laugh at myself and I laugh at him as well. We have our own little language and do funny voices. When we answer the phone to one another, we say 'hello' in a particular way. I hear Mollie doing something similar with her boyfriend, Andy, too. Oh God, if anyone saw us at home! We have our own thing and nobody else should ever witness it.

I met Ben around the time we did the Clothes Show Live, in December 2008. The Saturdays weren't big at that point, although we had released a couple of videos, and I was still travelling by bus and Tube without being recognised. Things were starting to change, though.

Ben, who is a rugby player, spotted me on the 'Up' video and a T4 interview, I think. Then he went on YouTube and watched all the videos. Next he went on our official website, which said I was in a relationship. 'Oh,' he thought, 'she has a boyfriend.' Only I didn't! I had broken up with my boyfriend months before that. It was just that the site hadn't been updated.

One day, Ben was speaking to his sports agent, who asked him if he fancied anyone.
— 'There's this gorgeous girl in this band called the Saturdays,' he said. 'Have you heard of them?'
— 'I think I've heard of them, yeah,' his agent replied.
— 'The Irish one. I really like her.'
When he heard this, his agent got a bit excited.
— 'You never know, I may be able to put a call in and see if she will go on a date with you,' he said. He didn't know anyone in my management, but he called the label and found out our press manager's number. His PR people spoke to our PR people and then our PR people sent me an email, saying, 'Very random. You are probably not interested, but this guy wants to go on a date with you.' They weren't going to send it at first, but they must have seen something in it. There was a small photo attached, along with his biog. It was like a CV for a relationship!

The biog said that Ben played for a club called Northampton Saints in Northampton, which I assumed was up north. Actually, it's not very far from London, but I knew nothing about the geography of England! 'He's up north?' I thought, 'so how am I ever going to see him?' I was also put off by his height, because he looked a bit short in the photo, standing next to his agent. Little did I know that he is six foot and only looked small because his agent is six foot seven!

I felt flattered that he had gone to the trouble of finding me. Plus, it's very hard in this industry to meet people. 'You know what?' I thought. I will go on a date with him!

— 'Why not?' I replied. 'Here's my number. Give it to him.' Shortly afterwards, he gave me a call. He didn't text me; he is quite forward! I didn't answer the phone, as I was in the next room, but I think he thought I'd just let it ring out. He left a voicemail saying,

— 'You must think this is a strange one, but I'd like to meet you for a drink . . .'

I called him back straight away and we were chatting away for the next half an hour.

— 'OK, I'm going to go now,' he said a couple of times.

— 'No, don't go,' I said. After that, we were constantly in touch, even before we met each other. We even discussed what we were going to do on New Year's Eve, before we physically met.

— 'What are you doing New Year's Eve?' I asked.

— 'I'm not sure. Do you want to do something?'

> IT'S SO NERVE-WRACKING WHEN YOU MEET SOMEONE FOR THE FIRST TIME, ESPECIALLY IF YOU HAVE BUILT THEM UP IN YOUR MIND! THANKFULLY, I KNEW I LIKED HIM THE MOMENT I MET HIM.
>
> UNA

It's so nerve-wracking when you meet someone for the first time, especially if you have built them up in your mind! I'd got on well with him and I liked what he looked like in the photo, but you never know how it's going to be in the flesh. Thankfully, I knew I liked him the moment I met him. It was a huge relief. Ben had only just started playing for England then, so it wasn't a case of thinking, 'Right, I'm in

a pop band, so I'll go out with an England rugby player.' Our careers didn't really take off until after we met each other. On our first date, he came to pick me up at my flat. My sister, Deirdre, was visiting me that weekend, and while I was getting ready, I heard them getting on really well. That's a bonus, I thought. It was definitely a good sign.

— 'I think I'm going to give him a kiss goodbye later!' I told her as I left.

We went out for dinner and a couple of drinks; we instantly hit it off. Then he dropped me home and gave me a kiss on the cheek. I might as well kiss you, I thought. When you like someone, I think the first kiss says it all and you might as well get it out of the way. There is no point going on a second date if the kiss doesn't go well. (It did go well!)

We jumped straight in after that. We've now bought a house together, we live together, and we've got two dogs! It's amazing how much my life has changed. I often think that, if I hadn't been in the band, I would never have met Ben, because he would never have seen me in that interview.

— 'You are the one,' he told me, very soon after we met. I never said it back to him, though. It's not that I don't think he is the one, but I don't think about it that way.

It's funny, because our paths nearly crossed once before, when I was playing a gig in Limerick and Ben's team came in. This was when he was playing for a team called Sale Sharks, near Manchester. Remembering this, I asked him,

— 'Weren't you there that night?'

— 'That was the one time in my life that I was injured!' he said. 'If I'd been there, I would definitely have come up and spoken to you.'

Everything went really fast. We met in December and were living together two and a half months later. I didn't have a car at the time, so he was driving to and from training in Northampton as often as he could. It got to the point when we asked each other,

— 'How much longer can we do this?'

We spent New Year's Eve together and on New Year's Day we sat discussing the situation.
— 'It would be so much easier if we had a base midway between London and Northampton,' Ben said. I looked at a map of England and saw that St Albans was about halfway, so that's where we moved first. We rented for a year before buying a house in the area.
ᵥᵥ

Ben still always says to all his friends, I've never felt like this about anyone. He is confident and certain of me, and I totally trust him. I never worry about what he's doing when I'm not there. We often spend nights apart. He goes on nights out without me, and I go on nights out without him.
ᵥᵥ

I've gone out with guys who gave me a reason to be worried, but I'm fine with Ben. I've never felt so comfortable with someone. I know he would never cheat on me.
ᵥᵥ

We got our first dog, Jackson, in August last year.

He's half pug, half Jack Russell. He was a bit lonely at first when we left him. I felt really sorry for him. When I said, 'Bye, Jackson!' in the mornings, his sorrowful expression broke my heart.
— 'We have to get him a friend,' we decided, so along came Bono, who is half pug, half Pomeranian.
ᵥᵥ

They are as thick as thieves now, really good friends. They're always playing and making noises and nibbling each other and play-fighting. It's just so lovely to see. I mainly have them in the house, because they're house dogs, but one day I let them out into the garden for some fresh air while I went for a shower. When I went to call them back in, they were gone! 'Oh God!' I thought. I was really worried, especially as it was raining.
ᵥᵥ

Jackson was the culprit, I think. He had dug under the back door and escaped! By the time I went to find them, little Bono was way down the road. He could easily have been killed by a car. Jackson was just out at the front of the house. He is more loyal,

I think, and knows not to wander too far. It was a real shock and I've now put bricks down so they can't get out again!

Rochelle — Some of the others were single when we formed the band, but I had a boyfriend, Darren. He played football for Charlton and I'd known him since I was fifteen, because we were in the same group of friends. I never really saw him in a romantic way back then, but we got together when I was seventeen and then it was on and off for a while.

Things were very up and down in the beginning. Because he wasn't around much, it would get to the point where I'd decide I would rather be on my own. Then he'd turn up and want to be with me and I'd say 'no' at first and then agree. Finally we stuck together; I started staying with him a lot and then we bought a two-bedroom house together last summer. It wasn't long before I started to get the feeling that it wasn't right. I felt haunted by what had happened at the start of our relationship and I constantly worried about where he was and what he was doing. On the other hand, I had known him for a long time from a young age; he was friends with my family; we got on really well and had the same group of friends. I thought it would be hard to find someone else I felt so comfortable with. It's difficult to know who is real and who isn't, especially in this business.

But being faithful is very important to me and, after a while, everything started freaking me out and I just couldn't do it any more. By December 2009, I knew it wasn't working for me. I didn't feel that he was interested in what I was doing and it all started to go downhill. So we decided to split up.

We are probably both to blame for things going wrong between us, and it's partly because things didn't start out right, I think. I hope Darren will always be one of my friends. It's slightly awkward right now, because it's still a bit raw, but I'd like to see us being friends in the future, I really would.

What made it more difficult was that, as soon as I split up with him, the press started saying, 'Rochelle is single!' Every time I went on a night out, it was shoved in his face. He's a footballer and they always have the papers, don't they? It's the first thing they see at training. I'd be pictured coming out of a club, possibly a bit tipsy, and the accompanying article would say something about me being with this guy or that guy, when I was simply out with my friends. I mean, I'd just broken up with my boyfriend! Being with someone else was the last thing on my mind.

I hated the thought of him constantly being reminded of me. No break-up is easy, whoever is responsible. It's like a death. It's the end of life as it was.In the months after we split up, I would text him: 'Just to give you a heads-up about what the papers are running. They're saying this and that, but it isn't true. I wasn't even in the UK at the time!' I wanted to warn him, out of respect for him. He would always have found out anyway, because we are in the same circle and a couple of my friends are good friends of his.

For a while, I was single. I just wanted to be on my own, get my head straight and concentrate on my career. This is why having a demanding job is so good, because when your relationship isn't going well or you go through something like a break-up, you can focus your attention somewhere else. It never affected my work; if anything, it made me work harder, so I could distract myself.

Then Marvin came along, which was a bit of a surprise. It was a nice surprise, of course, but it wasn't supposed to happen. Ideally, my plan was to stay single for a while, but as my mum said,
— 'The timing is never right.'

I had met Marvin and the JLS boys loads of times on the circuit. I always thought they were lovely, but that was it, even though Marvin made it clear that he liked me. When you have a boyfriend, you don't notice other men. It doesn't even enter your head to think of someone else.

> FOR A WHILE, I WAS SINGLE. I JUST WANTED TO BE ON MY OWN, GET MY HEAD STRAIGHT AND CONCENTRATE ON MY CAREER.
> ROCHELLE

As soon as Marvin knew I was single, he asked someone we both work with for my number. Straight away he called and said,
— 'Can I take you on a date?' I said 'no', because I didn't feel ready to go on a date. He kept asking me and I kept saying, 'No, no.' Then a friend asked me,
— 'Why won't you go on a date with him?'
— 'I don't know,' I answered.
— 'It's just a date. You're not getting married at dinner!'
— 'I suppose you're right,' I said hesitantly.
— 'Just go!'

So we went out and we got on very well. We took it slowly at the start, but things became serious quite quickly. We didn't play any games; we knew we liked each other and just took it from there. We saw each other all the time, as much as we could. He hung out at my work, I went to see him at his work and we stayed with each other every night, unless one of us was away. We missed each other so much when he was in LA that I went out to visit him for four days! We don't like being apart.

It's cool being with someone who is in the same business; we do exactly the same things for a living, so there's no need to justify or explain the job. It's really refreshing. Things have gone from strength to strength and every step we've taken has felt right – it hasn't felt like we're rushing things; it all feels very natural. We like the same things; he gets on really well with my family and friends and I get on well with his family and friends. We're totally compatible.

Now we're ready to move in together, we're looking for a house. I'm really looking forward to setting up home with Marvin; luckily, he's as tidy as I am!

Vanessa — I met my ex-boyfriend, Adam, through my school friend Matt. They were in a group that appeared on *The X Factor* a few years back. I remember Matt going on about Adam:
— 'He's such a great guy. You should meet him.'
— 'Yeah, yeah, whatever,' I said. I didn't think about it much, to be honest. I was so happy doing what I was doing, having fun with the girls and seeing my friends, that I wasn't bothered about boys. I was too busy for them.

I met him briefly for the first time the night we did a gig in Brighton, supporting Girls Aloud. There wasn't a big moment when we locked eyes and knew this was it; we just got on really well. I had never fallen in love before. Yes, I had teenage crushes, but I wasn't in love with anyone. It was just fun, whereas this was a serious relationship, my first true love. We had our ups and downs, though. We broke up for a few weeks,

then got back together, partly because it's hard to keep a relationship going when you are so busy.

A few of us had gone through break-ups and suddenly the press said,
— 'Finally, the Saturdays have split up with their boyfriends. Let's see what happens next.' I'd be out with my best friends, and some of my best friends are guys, and we'd link arms, because that's what good friends do.
— 'Who is Vanessa's hunky new man?' asked the papers.

'Oh, no, not him!' I'd think. 'He's my mate. Set me up with someone else!'
When I was younger, I used to think I would get married when I was around twenty-two and have a baby at around twenty-five. Now, I think, I am definitely not going to do that! In fact, I don't want a baby for a very long time. It's really weird how when you are younger you think twenty-five is so old. All of a sudden I'm twenty years old and I'm thinking, Not ready for that!

At the moment, I live with Mum, Dad and my brother. I'm hardly ever home, though, which is why I've lived there so long! I love my family, but I don't think I would still be living with them if I was at home all the time. When I was with Adam, I spent practically all my time at his house. My room at home wasn't a room any more. It was just a storage space full of suitcases and clothes that wouldn't fit into the wardrobe. I have three different-sized suitcases; when I go away, I just pull them out and chuck a few clothes in.

When Adam and I split up, my mum felt sorry for me and helped me clean everything up. There are still ridiculous amounts of clothes and shoes everywhere, but it's a lot neater than it was before. You can see the bed, at least!

I'm such a messy person that sometimes I can't find anything to wear. At times it's impossible to move around because there are clothes all over the bed and floor. My mum has warned me that she won't help me clean it any more. She doesn't see the point, because moments after she's finished it will be like a bomb has hit it. She keeps giving me hints about having the room back, but I pretend not to notice!

Mollie — I love being in love. If I like someone enough to go out with them, then they will be very important to me and I want them to feel the same way. I don't go out with someone just to have a boyfriend – I'm happy enough on my own spending time with girlfriends and my family, so someone has got to be really special for me to want to spend loads of time with them. Luckily, both the boys I have been out with so far have been really special.

I met my first boyfriend, Daniel, when I was out with my friend Charlotte. I was sixteen and he had just turned twenty-one. I spotted him out the corner of my eye and thought he was gorgeous. We kept looking at each other and, eventually, when I passed him on the stairs, he stopped me and chatted – he was lovely. He was over from South Africa on holiday but was actually half Italian and half Argentinian and believed that girls should be looked after and protected. – very old-fashioned, you might say, but I like that. Anyway, we got on really well and he never went back home. A real family boy, he got on well with my sisters and my mum and we stayed together for four years. He was really supportive with all my efforts to become a singer – he always thought I would make it and never stood in my way or laughed at me for having such big dreams. I have a lot to thank him for. But four years is a long time when you're young; I felt I needed to spread my wings a bit and, eventually, we decided to go our separate ways.

It was strange being on my own, after having a boyfriend for so many years; being single felt very strange. Bobbi, one of the Fallen Angelz, was to remedy that! She told me about one of her housemates, Andy, and showed me pictures of him. He looked cute and it sounded like we would have

THE PRESS
WERE STILL
CALLING ME
'MOLLIE, THE
SINGLE ONE IN
THE SATURDAYS'
MONTHS AFTER
I'D STARTED
GOING OUT
WITH ANDY,
BUT IT DIDN'T
BOTHER ME
MUCH.
MOLLIE

a lot in common, so we swapped numbers. He called me and we got on well on the phone.

∽

I was very nervous about meeting him the first time but Bobbi was there chatting away, so we hardly got a word in edgeways and I just kept looking at him, thinking 'you're so adorable!' We clicked right away. He is going to hate me for saying this but he went in for the kiss twice that evening and both times I gave him the cheek. I have only ever kissed three boys on the first night and I wasn't going to give in that easily – no matter how cute he was!

∽

After a few more dates, he asked me out and we've been together for a year and a half now. One of the things I liked about Andy straight away was that he is a musician, so we had a lot in common. He's in a band called Lawson and things are looking really good for them so I hope he gets the success that he deserves. It's great because Andy has been on tour with some big names and gigs a lot, too, so he understands the pressures and how tired I get sometimes. He gets a bit fed up with us not being able to go out without being papped though and I don't blame him – I would probably feel the same if it were the other way round!

∽

I love being with Andy, and until a few months ago, it was just the two of us; this was until my poodle Alfie came along and he insists on sitting between us on the sofa. Andy loves looking after Alfie, too, although he does always seem to be busy whenever Alfie does a poop. Typical boy hey?

∽

I do love having a boyfriend. When the Saturdays started, when I had just split up with Daniel and we went on tour with Girls Aloud, I really wanted to come off stage and call someone and tell them all about it. Of course, you can call your mum but it's not the same. Frankie was single, too, and we used to laugh together and say, 'We want a boyfriend!' But I'm not the type who wants to go out clubbing and living the single life – a different boy friend every

week! I love to be in love and sharing everything with someone special.

∽

Months after I started going out with Andy the press were still calling me 'Mollie, the single one' in the Saturdays but I didn't mind. I reckon I've been pretty lucky with the press so far and I still get excited when I see myself in newspapers and magazines. I'll always text my mum and dad, my sisters, my grandparents and my boyfriend to say 'Buy Heat! I'm in it!' Recently I texted them all to say that we were in the *News of the World*. My mum and my grandma texted back, 'I hope you've got clothes on!' 'Yes I have, thank you!' I replied. My mum keeps two scrapbooks – one for herself and one for me to look back on in years to come when it's all just memories.

> I RECKON I'VE BEEN PRETTY LUCKY WITH THE PRESS SO FAR AND I STILL GET EXCITED WHEN I SEE MYSELF IN NEWSPAPERS AND MAGAZINES. I'LL ALWAYS TEXT MY MUM AND DAD, MY SISTERS, MY GRANDPARENTS AND MY BOYFRIEND TO SAY 'BUY HEAT! I'M IN IT!'
> MOLLIE

There are times when it can be annoying to get snapped by the paps, especially if you know you're looking bad. One story that came out was when I had been blinded by flashbulbs and had tripped over the pavement. They implied that I had been drunk. The headline read something like 'One Too Many for Mollie.' Since I don't drink, it was irritating. But you can't call them up and say, 'Excuse me, I think you've made a mistake.' All you can do is post something on *Twitter* and have a laugh about it. It's not the end of the world!

UNA HEALY

WHEN YOU COME HOME FROM AN AUDITION THAT YOU DIDN'T GET, REMEMBER IT'S NOT THE END OF THE WORLD. DON'T GET DOWN ABOUT IT. JUST KEEP THINKING ABOUT THE NEXT AUDITION AND HOW YOU CAN DO BETTER WHEN IT COMES ROUND.

AGE — 29
BIRTH — 10 OCTOBER 1981
SIGN — LIBRA
FROM — IRELAND

About me — I am a get-up-and-go-girl. The opposite of laid back. I eat, drink, walk and talk fast. I like to be active, so I find it hard to just chill out, as I worry I haven't done something. I'm very passionate and like to speak my mind. You can have a row with me, but I never hold a grudge once it's sorted out. I feel so lucky to be doing what I love doing, while being given the opportunity to work with incredibly talented people whom I admire. Every day is different and exciting!

On small-town beginnings — Hopefully, people who come from small towns can look at me and be inspired, because I'm proof that you can come from a small town and make it. It's a bit harder, because the opportunities aren't there and you don't meet the right people so easily. You have to go out and find it yourself, so it's more of a struggle. It is possible, though, and I wouldn't swap the life I had growing up. I had a really normal, happy childhood.

Are you a good shopper? — I hate shopping. I never try anything on. The mirrors and the lights in dressing rooms are never very flattering, so everything is going to look awful anyway. I generally know if something is going to fit by holding it up against myself. If I don't like it straight away, I won't buy it, but certain things catch my eye. I know what size I am and it's not often that I buy something that doesn't fit. If it does happen, I just give it to someone else. I don't buy a lot, so I don't do huge, massive shopping sprees.

I AM A GET-UP-AND-GO-GIRL. THE OPPOSITE OF LAID BACK. I EAT, DRINK, WALK AND TALK FAST.

Red-carpet tips? — Mollie and I have a laugh on the red carpet when she sees me doing that over-the-shoulder look and I see her doing the pout. We all laugh at each other. Some people say, 'Why do you never smile for photos? You look so miserable.' Well, sometimes I don't like looking cheesy, so I do a little pout. I can't help it!

I HAD MY HEART BROKEN WHEN I WAS YOUNG. YOU JUST NEED TO CRY IT ALL OUT. THERE IS NO SHAME IN CRYING. IT'S ALSO GOOD TO TALK AND TALK AND TALK ABOUT IT, BECAUSE YOU NEED TO GET IT OUT OF YOUR SYSTEM!

Five words that describe me best

—

Artistic
Determined
Outgoing
Romantic
Feisty

Favourite Saturdays video?

—

The 'Just Can't Get Enough' video was very easy and relaxing to make. I love it because there's something different happening in every shot.

Most embarrassing moment

—

Sending a text message about somebody to the wrong person; it left me with a lot of explaining to do!

On flirting

—

My advice would be to listen a bit more than you normally would and don't talk too much. Don't drift off; ask questions; make sure you seem interested.

Fashion advice?
—
I just wear whatever I want. I only worry if I turn up somewhere and feel over- or underdressed. Otherwise, I don't ever really worry about what I wear.

Favourite Saturdays single?
—
I love 'Ego.'

For me, it's one of those songs you could never get sick of.

Favourite items in my wardrobe
—
Fave jeans
Flip-flops
(weather permitting)
Numerous vest tops
Leather jackets

I'M NOT A FLIRTATIOUS PERSON, UNLIKE FRANKIE, WHO ADMITS TO BEING THE BIGGEST FLIRT IN THE WORLD. SHE IS VERY TACTILE AND TOUCHES PEOPLE WHEN SHE SPEAKS TO THEM. MY ADVICE WOULD BE TO LISTEN A BIT MORE THAN YOU NORMALLY WOULD AND DON'T TALK TOO MUCH.

On looking sexy — When we're on stage and I look around at us all trying to be sexy, it looks really ridiculous.

Do you want to get married? — I will get married one day, but not for a while. I haven't been asked yet, so I can't really say when! But I don't want to do it anytime soon. When I do get married, I am going to have a very big wedding. I come from a massive family; I've got more than sixty cousins, so family weddings are always huge.

What's your style? — Dressy casual. Obviously, on a big night I love to wear lovely dresses and heels. During the day I prefer just jeans and Nike fitted T-shirts and Ugg boots, with flip-flops and maxi-dresses in the summer. At home, I take everything off and just put on my comfy tracksuit bottoms and my hoodie. That is the way I am at home.

Dating tips? — I always put on good music when I'm getting ready. I dance in front of the mirror and have mock conversations with myself. Practise a little bit what you are going to say and do, so that you have a few things up your sleeve. Then you won't go in thinking, 'What am I going to say?'

Flirting tips? — I'm not a flirtatious person, unlike Frankie, who admits to being the biggest flirt in the world. She is very tactile and touches people when she speaks to them. My advice would be to listen a bit more than you normally would and don't talk too much. Don't drift off; ask questions; make sure you seem interested. Obviously, it can go too far. I've been out with guys and spent the whole date listening to them, which is so boring! You want someone to be interested in you as well.

Rejection remedy? — I had my heart broken when I was young. There is nothing that will heal it but time. You just need to cry it all out. There is no shame in crying. It's also good to talk and talk and talk about it, because you need to get it out of your system! It helps to be around the people who love you and will listen to you. Don't go too wild. People may advise you to go out all the time to get over it, but inevitably you'll get to that certain point in the night where you start missing them or feeling sorry for yourself when you see other couples. So I don't think it's a good thing to socialise too much immediately after a break-up. In fact, I think it makes it harder.

When you come home from an audition that you didn't get, remember it's not the end of the world. Don't get down about it. Just keep thinking about the next audition and how you can do better when it comes round.

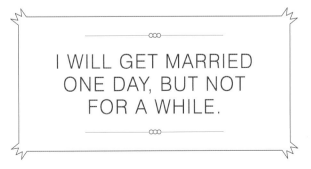

I WILL GET MARRIED ONE DAY, BUT NOT FOR A WHILE.

2004
♪ Overall Winner:
One Thousand Euro

THE SATURDAYS

Style Secrets

Looking good is part of the job and over the
years we have begged, borrowed and stolen
all sorts of beauty and style secrets from the
professionals who work their magic on us.
Here are a few of our favourites...

'If you smudge a nail just after you've painted it, wet your finger and smooth it over.'

Top Beauty Tips

Una
—
If I wear fake tan, like Mollie and I do quite
a lot of the time, make sure you put plenty
of moisturiser on your wrists, knuckles, knees
and ankles before you apply it. If you don't,
the fake tan catches in the creases of your
joints, which is a dead giveaway.

Frankie

Always take your make-up off
before you go to bed, so that
your skin is clean and can
breathe while you're asleep.

Mollie
—
Apply a touch of concealer or
foundation to your eyelids before
putting on your eyeshadow. It makes it
stay on longer. But never wear heavy
eye make-up with a strong lip colour,
as it's just too much!

Rochelle
—
If you smudge a nail just after you've
painted it, wet your finger and smooth
it over. The nail varnish goes back into
place!

Vanessa
—
Sometimes I leave a Kerastase conditioning
treatment in my hair all night. It really helps
combat the damage done by blow drying, tonging and
straightening. I also drink a lot of water, which
helps to keep your skin clear.

On a desert island I could not do without...

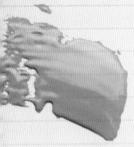

Vanessa

—

My Mac lipstick — it's an orange-red colour and it's called 'Lady Danger!'

Frankie

—

False lash effect mascara, it makes such a difference.

Rochelle

—

My Crème de la Mer tinted moisturiser. I like it because it's got a bit of coverage, but it's not a foundation, so it's very light.

Mollie

—

Elizabeth Arden Eight Hour Cream. I'm addicted to having soft lips and it's a lifesaver, especially on the beach.

Una

—

You want to look natural on a beach, so it would have to be my Luminous Silk Foundation by Giorgio Armani. You can't tell you're wearing it and yet it gives you a flawless complexion.

'I'm addicted to having soft lips and it's a lifesaver, especially on the beach'

229

'I've definitely grown in confidence now, so I put on whatever I feel comfortable in'

Biggest Mistake

Vanessa
—

I felt like I was always making mistakes when I was young, but I've definitely grown in confidence now, so put on whatever I feel confortable in!

Rochelle
—

On one of the first ever test shoots for the Saturdays, the make-up artist gave me bright orange lipstick and crimped hair. I looked like a 1980s throwback, something out of a really scary movie!

Frankie
—

Twice I used eyelash curlers and they chopped off my eyelashes! I had to wear false eyelashes until they grew back, so I stay away from eyelash curlers now.

Una
—

I once put a dark brown dye in my hair and it came out jet black! I washed it about a hundred times to get it out. Now I always choose a colour that looks a few shades lighter on the packet than the colour I actually want, because it always comes out darker.

Mollie
—

I've always looked the same since I was ten — blonde with a centre parting. But earlier in the year I tried having a fringe, which was something I had been contemplating for months. I wanted it to be heavy and chunky, but my hair is fine, although thick, so it ended up looking a bit wispy. A fringe didn't suit my face either. It made me look harder, which isn't the image I'm going for!

THE SATURDAYS
MOVING FORWARD

BEFORE WE KNEW IT, WE WERE RECORDING OUR SECOND ALBUM, *WORDSHAKER*, WHICH WAS RELEASED IN OCTOBER 2009, ALONG WITH A NEW SINGLE, 'FOREVER IS OVER'. THIS TIME AROUND, WE HAD MORE INPUT IN THE MUSIC AND STYLING OF THE BAND, WHICH MADE THINGS EVEN MORE FUN AND EXCITING THAN EVER! WHAT A WHIRLWIND THREE YEARS IT HAS BEEN... BUT WHAT WILL THE FUTURE HOLD?

Rochelle — The second album came around very quickly. It felt as though we had only just released *Chasing Lights* when we performed it on tour and then suddenly we were in the studio recording *Wordshaker*. It was so much fun, though. We went to LA to record some of the songs, which was unreal. It is such a different way of working there. It was hot, it was sunny, and when I came out of the recording booth, I'd pass two of the girls sunbathing.

We were there for a couple of weeks, but it seemed like for ever, in a good way. I loved it. We stayed in an amazing rented house and spent our time going shopping or out for dinner. Jordan, our A&R man, was in LA at the time. He's twenty-three and we get on really well. He lives near me in Essex now and he often pops over, or we'll go out with my friends, his girlfriend and her friends. It was so much fun having him out there. Although technically he is my boss, it didn't feel like it. We made him take us out for dinner and to a club.

> WE WENT TO LA TO RECORD SOME OF THE SONGS, WHICH WAS UNREAL
> ROCHELLE

Because he is young, he wanted to do the same stuff as us. Guess who called us and asked if we would go out for dinner with him? David Hasselhoff. It was so funny. He was nice.
— 'It was so lovely to meet you girls,' he said.
— 'Really?' I said. 'Lovely to meet you too.'

Mollie — When we made our first album, we didn't really know each other. We recorded it even before going on tour with Girls Aloud.

When it came to recording the second album, though, we knew each other really, really well; we were also more experienced and grown-up. We also had more say over which songs were used. With the first album, I felt quite down because I didn't sing as much as I wanted to, but now I realise that when you are in a band with someone like Vanessa, it is completely right that she should be singing the majority of the songs. I tend to sing the softer parts. After all, I could be belting all day, but I'm never going to be belting as loud as Vanessa. She is incredible.

On *Chasing Lights* we were developing the Saturdays' sound and musical genre. When it came to recording *Wordshaker*, we had more power to say which songs we liked and the ones we weren't as keen on. So we really like every song on *Wordshaker*. We released two fantastic singles from the album: 'Forever Is Over', which reached number two, and 'Ego', which was number nine.

Vanessa — We had a bit more input when it came to the second album, but it's not like we haven't always been very outspoken! Right from the start we had strong ideas about what we did and didn't like. Still, we did contribute more on the second album. I love writing songs. I write them on my own in my bedroom.

One of my songs was the basis for one of our B-sides. I wrote it before I got into the band and put it up on my MySpace. It was there for ages, just as an acoustic, and then I asked one of my friends, a talented producer, to work on it. We changed it a bit and I played it to the girls, who really liked it. Then we all started adding to it and changing bits, so it became more of a collective effort. Everyone contributed and made changes, which was fun. Even the name changed from 'Artificial' to 'Unofficial' and then it became the B-side of 'Work'. All the girls enjoy writing songs, especially when we're together. Just put us in a room and we come up with ideas.

It was a good experience and now I want to do more. When we are busy, though, I don't have much time to write or experiment, which is really annoying. My friends are all singers and we often used to get together and write together and mess about. I feel like I want to do that again. I miss those sessions.

Rochelle — When I hear a song for the first time, I visualise everything to do with it: the video, the performance, the live performance – literally everything. My brain is ticking over creatively and I like to be hands-on with decisions about presentation, styling and make-up.

In the beginning, it wasn't quite the same, because when you start a project, it's good to be given some direction. We are five individuals; we needed to be taken somewhere so that we could develop and build on what we had together. I think that's why we

WHEN I HEAR
A SONG FOR
THE FIRST TIME,
I VISUALISE
EVERYTHING
TO DO WITH IT:
THE VIDEO, THE
PERFORMANCE,
THE LIVE
PERFORMANCE
– LITERALLY
EVERYTHING.
ROCHELLE

WE'RE AT A GREAT STAGE JUST NOW BECAUSE WE'RE HAPPY WITH WHAT WE HAVE ACHIEVED SO FAR.

UNA

didn't write the first album. We needed to find our direction first. Once we had done that and hit the nail on the head with help from the label, it became much easier to be hands-on.

This is the stage I wanted to get to. We used to have a lot more help, but now we're asked, 'Girls, what do you think of this?' We have more opportunity to tweak things.

We recorded some of the tracks on the first album within the first few weeks of being together. I love those tracks and they are Saturdays tracks – they bring back good memories of when we first got together – but they don't necessarily represent all of us.

We didn't write loads of the songs on the second album, but we chose them, and we picked them because they meant something to us. So although the first album is equally as important to us, our second album feels a lot more personal.

Una — We're at a great stage just now because we're happy with what we have achieved so far. We've had some good hits and we are working on new material at the moment, getting more involved in the writing process.

We've got the chance to contribute more to the music because we actually have some time to write now. I craved that more than anything right from the start. I waited so long for a break and worked so hard for it. It has all paid off in the end.

Rochelle — I'll never forget Emma Bunton saying, 'Just try and take it in, because you will be so busy, you will forget.' We met her when we did her Heart FM radio show and she went on to say that she had forgotten some of the things she had done with the

Spice Girls. 'I see a picture and I have to try hard to remember where we were,' she added.

It's hard to take things in when you are flying around and gearing up to do something different every day. Although everything is fun, it is work, and sometimes there isn't even time to say, 'How good was that yesterday?' Often it's only much later that you realise how amazing it was, although we try and make a point of taking the time to talk about everything.

> # I WAITED SO LONG FOR A BREAK AND WORKED SO HARD FOR IT. IT HAS ALL PAID OFF IN THE END.
>
> UNA

Frankie — Performing is second nature to me. It's something I'm used to and it kind of feels as if I couldn't do anything else now. It's all I know, which is quite scary. When I was in S Club Juniors, I wasn't as aware of myself as I am now. When you're young, you're just really confident; you do your stuff without thinking about it. But now that I'm older, I'm conscious that what I do is a career, not just something I've ended up doing that gets me out of going to school. I get more nervous these days. I'm much more aware of my situation than I was. Also, the music industry has completely changed since I was in S Club Juniors, so I'm learning how everything works all over again.

Music has become much more Internet-based in the last few years. The Saturday-morning TV shows have disappeared, along with loads of the pop magazines. Woolworths has gone, too, and it used to be the place where we bought CDs. Because of

WE OFTEN FORGET
THAT WE'VE
BEEN TOGETHER
MORE THAN
THREE YEARS.
IT'S QUITE A
LONG TIME,
BUT IT FEELS
LIKE NO MORE
THAN A YEAR.
THE YEARS GO
BY SO QUICKLY!
UNA

WE ALL HAVE OUR OWN REASONS FOR WANTING TO BE AS BIG AS WE CAN. NOW THAT WE KNOW EACH OTHER SO WELL, WE SHOULDER RESPONSIBILITIES TOGETHER, SO IF ANYTHING GOES WRONG, THEN IT'S SOMETHING WE ALL GO THROUGH.

FRANKIE

Twitter and Facebook and MySpace, singers and performers are far more accessible than they used to be and as a result there's not so much excitement around them any more.

o–

In one way that's good, because people don't have an unrealistic view of who you are and the idea of doing something for themselves is much more possible, but on the other hand it kind of ruins it, because there's a little less stardust around performers. They're not the idols they used to be, which makes them less exciting; there was much more hysteria surrounding the whole thing when I was younger.

o–

When we were younger, pop stars were more spoiled, whereas we were getting the Tube for ages when the Saturdays started up. That was fine; it didn't bother me at all, and it's probably a good thing, because people don't get ahead of themselves.

o–

A lot of kids now want to be famous for no reason, or they want to marry a footballer and live a life of luxury. I think that's a bit of a shame. They don't seem to realise how much hard work it takes to be in a band.

PERFORMING IS SECOND NATURE TO ME.
IT'S SOMETHING I'M USED TO AND IT KIND OF FEELS AS IF I COULDN'T DO ANYTHING ELSE NOW.

FRANKIE

Although I was lucky enough to be in the right place at the right time, we still had to work for it

o–

I was always aware that I didn't want to be 'a childhood star', one of those mums who says, 'I was in a band when I was twelve.'
—'Oh, what happened?'
—'Nothing happened after that.'
Now that I'm older, I'm aware that it is a job. It's not just a bit of fun. I want to make enough money out of it so that hopefully I won't have to worry when I'm older, although I do want to work for years. That's my aim and I think it's the same for all of us. I want to do as much as I can now, at a young age, so that when I'm older, I can relax and not have to worry about money.

o–

We all feel the same way. Una worked really hard for years in Ireland, but her break just didn't come at first. Now that she's got it, she doesn't want to let it go. Mollie has always been obsessed with pop music and Britney, so this was her childhood dream. Rochelle has the same approach that I do, I think. As for Vanessa, she just loves singing. She's not necessarily into the promotion or the nights out, but she loves being a singer; she's had that massive voice from a very early age. So we all have our own reasons for wanting to be as big as we can.

o–

Now that we know each other so well, we shoulder responsibilities together, so if anything goes wrong, then it's something we all go through. You think, OK, that didn't go well. Let's all work together to make it work next time. We are very good like that. We understand that we need to work together, otherwise it's not going to happen.

We don't have time to argue. There is just no point. We would all hate our jobs if we argued; things wouldn't work out for us. We have never had a massive argument. We all love what we are doing and want the band to be the best it can. We are so focused on what we want to do that we really get on, even though we spend every day with each other. We've become like sisters.

Una — We often forget that we've been together more than three years. It's quite a long time, but it feels like no more than a year.

The years go by so quickly! In another three years, we'll have been together six years, which is the usual lifetime of a girl band. So if you think about it, we may be halfway through the journey already, which is a scary thought.

But maybe we'll have another go at it later, like Take That. Maybe in eight years we will come back and do it all again. That would be great!

In the meantime I've been working hard on my songwriting skills; I've written a song with Guy Chambers, who co-wrote the Robbie Williams song 'Angels,' and Gary Barlow invited me to Bath to take part in a songwriting workshop for female writers, which was amazing.

> ## WHAT DOES THE FUTURE HOLD? I WANT TO DO EVERYTHING. WE ALL DO.
> VANESSA

Vanessa — What does the future hold? I want to do everything. We all do. We want to go to Europe, then really crack Asia and the US after that. In the UK, we want to tour again and go on releasing singles and having fun. As long as we continue to do that, we'll all be very happy!

> ## I'M LOOKING FORWARD TO THE NEXT TOUR, BECAUSE PERFORMING IS WHAT I LOVE BEST. WE ALL DO. MEETING OUR FANS IS ONE OF THE NICEST PARTS OF OUR JOB
> MOLLIE

Mollie — I absolutely love every minute of this job! I think I'm the luckiest person in world. Every night I go to sleep looking forward to the next day at work and every morning I jump out of bed full of anticipation.

Frankie — I'd love us to get to the point where we become household names!

Mollie — There's lots to be excited about. Most of all, I'm looking forward to the next tour, because performing is what I love best. We all do. Meeting our fans is one of the nicest parts of our job – and going on tour is the best way to meet and get to know our fans.

Rochelle — The future is really exciting. At the time of writing this book we are preparing to release a mini album called Headlines. We had recorded some new material for a new album due out in 2011, but we couldn't wait that long for people to hear it. Missing You is our eighth single and it felt so summery, we wanted to release it right away. I hope we are still writing and recording together for a long time, because we really do have so much fun together.

> ## I ABSOLUTELY LOVE EVERY MINUTE OF THIS JOB! I THINK I'M LUCKIEST PERSON IN WORLD.
> ROCHELLE

TEN OUT OF TEN
FOR IMAGINATION!

We've lost our old school reports, or mislaid them, or whatever (ahem!), but we just love being nostalgic about the good old days of double maths and biology, lol! Here's what our teachers would have written about us if they were being totally honest . . .

— Year 2010 —

NAME *FRANKIE SANDFORD*

CLASS *THE SATURDAYS*   SCHOOL YEAR

SUBJECT	TEACHER'S COMMENTS

MATHS

Try harder! Frankie has never understood decimal points or percentages and she doesn't even pretend to! She makes it obvious how much she hates maths, and I'm constantly having to tell her off for talking in class.

ENGLISH

Top marks! She likes reading, loves writing essays and stories, and enjoys the drama of a good plot.

SCIENCE

7/10: quite good. She enjoys what she calls the 'fun stuff with the Bunsen burner' and hasn't blown anything up yet, luckily. She should really work harder on the theory of science, but I don't hold out a lot of hope!

ART

4/10: Frankie is good at craftwork, but her drawing skills are, frankly, terrible!

SPORT

What she lacks in skill, she makes up for in determination. Once again she has been selected for the trampolining and cross-country squads, but her rounders is slightly substandard. I keep telling her that she can hit the ball harder and further! For some reason, she chooses the basketball team over the netball team – it wouldn't be something to do with boys, would it? Still, as I said, I respect Frankie's determination, especially during cross-country runs, when she refuses to stop running, even when held up by a car!

CONCEN -TRATION

Good for about forty-five minutes.

GENERAL BEHAVIOUR

She is sociable and generally well behaved, although she often gets distracted and should concentrate more. The only time she's ever really been in trouble and we've had to give her a detention was when she forgot her homework diary. She must learn to be more organised. And although quite mischievous, she is never very naughty. The one thing she really needs to avoid is talking in class!

YOUR CHILD IS ASSIGNED TO, PROMOTED TO, RETAINED IN THE *SATURDAYS* GRADE

FOR THE SCHOOL YEAR *2010* SIGNATURE OF TEACHER

NAME *MOLLIE KING*

AGE

CLASS *THE SATURDAYS*

SCHOOL YEAR

SUBJECT	TEACHER'S COMMENTS
MATHS	It would be appreciated if Mollie could try to understand that "what's a calculator for then?" is not a reason not to learn long division.
ENGLISH	Mollie's stories are wild! Her stories are wild and whacky and full of imagination. Where does she get her ideas from?
SCIENCE	Mollie's endless love for animals has caused problems in the biology lab, none so irritating as when she freed all the spiders we had got in for observation because they were "cute".
ART	I would advise Mollie not to try drawing anything more complicated than stick men, because she just doesn't have any sense of perspective!
BUSINESS STUDIES	Mollie enjoys this subject and is always asking questions – when she means business, she means business. You certainly can't pull the wool over this pupil's eyes.
COOKERY	Not one of Mollie's strong points. Although quite inventive with baked beans, Mollie is better at salads or anything that comes ready to put on a plate. With her desire to eat healthily she might do well to make sure her boyfriend is a good cook.
SPORT	Mollie is our School Sports Captain and won the school sports scholarship - this is definitely her best subject!
GENERAL BEHAVIOUR	If chatting were a school subject she'd be top of the class! She seems to have found herself a nice group of very close friends, but the incessant giggling is going to have to stop! She is a good worker but her excuses for handing in her homework late are starting to wear thin. But we were very sorry to hear about the death of her 7th grandmother.

YOUR CHILD IS ASSIGNED TO, PROMOTED TO, RETAINED IN THE *SATURDAYS* GRADE

FOR THE SCHOOL YEAR *2010* SIGNATURE OF TEACHER

NAME _ROCHELLE WISEMAN_   AGE ____

CLASS _THE SATURDAYS_   SCHOOL YEAR ____

SUBJECT	TEACHER'S COMMENTS

MATHS

If she spent as much time concentrating on her binary equations as she does on her dancing and singing, she would be an A-star student! Unfortunately, this is not the case.

ENGLISH

Very good. Her creative stories and poetry are excellent.

SCIENCE

Rochelle is definitely a character and she always livens up the science laboratory. She's very entertaining but never gets on with her work, unless we're doing experiments with Bunsen burners, which she seems to enjoy, perhaps for the wrong reasons!

ART

She is an A-star student in art. Her portraits of her friends are excellent!

SPORT

Rochelle is good at running, cross-country and high jump, but we get a lot of letters from her mum asking if she can be excused from sport. Coincidentally, her mother's writing looks a lot like her best friend's!

GENERAL BEHAVIOUR

Rochelle is too conscientious to be very naughty, but she can't seem to help talking in class. She thinks she gets away with it, but, like most teachers, I really have got eyes in the back of my head! If she could stop gabbing and listen to what I'm saying, she might do very well, but she has lots of friends and is very sociable, so I'm probably asking too much.

YOUR CHILD IS ASSIGNED TO, PROMOTED TO, RETAINED IN THE _SATURDAYS_   GRADE

FOR THE SCHOOL YEAR _2010_ SIGNATURE OF TEACHER ____

NAME _UNA HEALY_

CLASS _THE SATURDAYS_   AGE

SCHOOL YEAR

SUBJECT	TEACHER'S COMMENTS
MATHS	A hundred per cent! That extra tuition at home has paid off! But she still chats too much in class and can be annoyingly cheeky.
ENGLISH	As I told her mother, Una needs to stop reading scary Stephen King novels. She claims she hasn't read a single one of his books, in which case she should stop watching gruesome films, because her stories are horrifying!
SCIENCE	This is a strong subject for Una, mainly, I suspect, because her much more scientifically minded sister gives her extra tuition at home!
ART	Sometimes she's a bit sloppy and rushes her work, but if she puts her mind to it, she can do an amazing job.
SPORT	Una is a very good hockey player and generally very good at sport.
CONCEN-TRATION	Her concentration definitely has a limit. She can be very well behaved for a short span and then she switches off and starts daydreaming. I suspect that she has filled whole exercise books with doodles!
GENERAL BEHAVIOUR	Una is very cheeky and bold, always in trouble, but essentially harmless. I've heard her described in the staffroom as a 'lovable rogue', which seems apt. When she is bored, she tends to stir up trouble and play the clown among her friends.

YOUR CHILD IS ASSIGNED TO, PROMOTED TO, RETAINED IN THE _SATURDAYS_ GRADE

FOR THE SCHOOL YEAR _2010_ SIGNATURE OF TEACHER

NAME _VANESSA WHITE_ ———————————————— AGE ————

CLASS _THE SATURDAYS_ ———————————— SCHOOL YEAR ————

SUBJECT	TEACHER'S COMMENTS

MATHS

Not Vanessa's best subject, which is why she has a home tutor. She needs to focus on doing extra work and concentrating.

ENGLISH

She's not the greatest at English language, but she deserved her B in English literature. Alarmingly, she tells me that Martina Cole is her favourite author and she loves the drama of the criminal underworld! She is also a huge fan of vampire stories on screen, including Vampire Diaries, Buffy and the Twilight films. She doesn't understand the obsession with Robert Pattinson, though – whoever he is!

SCIENCE

Vanessa has requested permission to drop this subject and I am allowing it, even though it is a compulsory subject. Science and Vanessa are not a good combination, unfortunately!

ART

Why, oh why can Vanessa never be bothered to put time and effort into her work? Her drawings can be quite good sometimes, but I suspect she is tracing them at home!

SPORT

She is a very good runner. Sometimes I wonder if she's going to run away and never come back!

CONCEN-TRATION

Terrible! She often can't be bothered to listen. And yet, strangely, some things completely fascinate her, in which case she will focus intensely. However, it is very hard to keep her attention. She is something of a mystery to me.

GENERAL BEHAVIOUR

She is extremely naughty and is often sent out of class for talking. Again and again I tell her to stop, but she won't cease her chatting!

YOUR CHILD IS ASSIGNED TO, PROMOTED TO, RETAINED IN THE _SATURDAYS_ GRADE

FOR THE SCHOOL YEAR _2010_ SIGNATURE OF TEACHER ————————————

THE SATURDAYS